NOT JUST A NUMBER

My Journey
into the Heart of
Modern-Day Slavery

NEKIESHA LYNN

Not Just a Number

Copyright © 2017 Nekiesha Lynn

This is a work of non-fiction. All conversations, places and people come from the author's recollections. Not all dialogue is a word-for-word transcription, rather, a retelling that accurately portrays the conversations that took place.

ISBN-13: 978-0692984017

First Edition: December 2017

www.nekieshalynn.com

Dedication

This book is dedicated to every person who has given financially. The stories you find on these pages is your legacy. Your finances were the tool that began the greatest work of all: the transformation of the soul. You have modeled through words and deeds I am not just a number.

We have stood together in the fight against modern-day slavery, human exploitation and sex trafficking. Your generosity will forever live on in the hearts of those directly impacted and those who read this book.

Abide Inc, Abraham Heating and Air Conditioning, Kaio & Leah Ahhing, Donald Allison, Alofa Tunoa Church American Samoa,

Antioch Church in Iliili American Samoa,
Steve & Barb Barney, Les & Kris Beauchamp,
Rick & Renea Berry, Connie Bissen, Richard Black,
Tony & Dawn Bouquet, Richard & Marilyn Bright,
Jonny & Debbie Buckner,
Robert Burdett, Brett & Julie Cain,
Community Christian Church American Samoa,
Jonah Kapono Chun, Calvin & Carol Cohnkey,
Karen & Thomas Cote, CUSP, Shaun & Jodie Deane,
Jeannine DeVetter, Brandon J. Dotzler,
Brett & JR Dotzler, David & Sandra Dotzler,
Jan C. Dotzler, Eric & Jessica Dotzler,
Paul & Julie Dotzler, Jay Dotzler
Ray Jr and Jan Dotzler, Raymond Sr. & Delores Dotzler,
Ron and Twany Dotzler, Stephanie Dotzler,
Taylea Dotzler, Jonathan Dotzler,
Krehauna Dotzler, Myhiah Dotzler,
Dr. Bernie & Debbie Douglas, Michelle Earhart,
Julie Erickson, Alexander Evans, Pina Faulkner,
Brian Feregrino, Michael Feregrino,
Dennis & Cynthia Fields, Steven and Michele Flott,
Andy and Leone Forsgren, Katie mar Frankl,
Jessica Gallant, Troy & Ruth Gentiles,
Mary-Helen, Dennis Goeschel,
Terrence & Barbara Graeve, Kieth & Kristy Gregerson,
Ana Hagett, Roger Harders,

Wilbur & Sylvia Hawley, Dr. Irene Helsham,
Donald & Michelle Hemsley, Kristin Hermann,
Jerrad & Julie Hertzler, Viliamu & Taimane Hollister,
Marva Holt, Jerome Hough, Audrey Hubbard,
Kristen Huff, Howard & Joan Hunter,
Brent & Jennifer Jackson, Garrett Jackson,
Jim Jackson, Lillian Jackson, Wallace Jennings,
Cyndi Johnson, Alexander & Janine Jones ,
Elisapeta Fa'alafi Jones, Dr. Glendell Jones,
Terry Kaser, Katina Missions, Joe & Lori Katina,
Keeler & Associates, Michael Kingery,
Brad & Julie Knutson, Patrick & Jean Lanphier,
Ling Li, Myrna Librojo,
Lifegate Church Omaha NE, Bethany Loux,
Josie Lutali, Lonnie & Jackie Mahr,
Moru & Sallie Mane, Michael Martin,
Art & Isabel Martinez, A.J. &·Veronica Martinez,
Donna Mayhan, Cameron Menneroh,
Chaundra Miller, John Murray,
Nativia Construction, Lexi Nelson,
Ronald & Jeanne Niederhaus, Fred & Fran Niedo,
Alaina Nielson, Solomona Nuusa,
Vai & Repeka Nuusa, Gary & Toni Olson,
Othiniel Otineru, Eugene & Lafoaina Palyo,
Tim & Peggy Parys, Kandas Paulson,
Kelly Petersen, Gary & Maralyn Phillips,

Myron & Kristen Pierce
Paul & Ana Rase, Frances Reed, Tim & Randie Reilly,
Rob Reuss, Don & Helen Richardson,
Anahi Salazar-Angulo,
Tess Sawan, Tyler & Theresa Schenzel,
Michael & Judy Schinker, Ron Schroeder,
Debra Scott, Wanda Selzer, Moelilia Seui,
Dennis & Debbie Snipes, Lori Spath, Harvey Springer,
Jonathan & Katja Starkey, Stein Construction,
Elizabeth Suwanto-Goh, Ethan & Michelle Svehla,
Faafetai Tago, Newington & Havilah Tamalii,
Tone & Ruta Tamalii, Richard & Debra Tesarek,
Larry & Leisha Timm, True North Trading Company,
Sarah Marie Vacha, Vip & Carrie Vipperman,
Saili Visan, Clinton & Jamie Veren,
Dane & Coco Watts, Mark & Rhonda Watts,
Larry & Barb Welchert, James & Paula Wells,
Sipopo S. Wilson, Gene Woodard,
Word of Life American Samoa,
Worship Center American Samoa,
Florence C Wysuph, Talei Nuusa,
Ledua & Mapper

...and the many more who gave.

Contents

chapter one

NOT JUST A NUMBER

People pushed and shoved, some shuffled slowly and some hurried. It was a mass of sweaty bodies packed like sardines that, somehow, kept moving. The walking space was not very big. There was one line each direction. Cars and motorbikes whizzed by too close for comfort. An occasional horn honked. Bodies were packed so tightly, I couldn't see much except all that was directly in front of me. Night had fallen, but the dark held deception.

So many people were out. Lights blared all around me and the neon signs blinded me. Spirit houses were adorned and decorated in Christmas lights. The noise—it was unbearably loud. People were speaking in many languages, but I could not understand anything they were saying.

On top of all the voices, the disco music blared. I

could feel the intensity vibrating through my body. I remember the cracked concrete on the ground dotted with oil spills, dirt and trash discarded carelessly on the floor—*lots* of trash.

There is a distinct smell in Thailand; it is the smell of fish oil being used in food dishes cooked on the side of the street in the open air. I inhaled the thick musky air as I continued to walk. I silently observed the many cultures around me. There were dark-skinned Africans, people of Middle Eastern origin, Eastern Europeans and many more I could not identify. I felt like a small fish in a great unfamiliar ocean. I could not help but be reminded of how far from home I was.

As I continued my walk, I tried to make sure I did not fall as I weaved around people, stepping up and down off the curb. It struck me as odd that so many people around me were women. They were from other nations and they wore towering heels and skirts two sizes too small. I felt uncomfortable seeing their scantily clad bodies. Many were clustered together in huddles.

Finally, the sea of people parted and I had arrived. I walked through an opening between two buildings. The lighted signs on the front of the buildings were just as loud and obnoxious as the noise. My body vibrated with every beat that echoed. Once I passed the buildings it was quieter, but my heart was racing faster than the motorbikes that zoomed by just moments ago.

What have I gotten myself into?

I stared at what looked like an enclosed compound type of building. I was standing in the middle of an opening. The air was thick around me, squeezing the breath out of me. I couldn't help but shiver, but I wasn't sure if it was from the nerves, or the iciness of my surroundings. The atmosphere was solemn. I didn't dare talk. There was nothing to say.

I came with a few others and we were debriefed before arriving. I had been instructed not to talk at all and just follow, so I obliged. I was enthralled in my own emotions and feelings. I didn't have anything to say to anyone in that moment. If this had been a temple or sacred place, one could imagine the stillness in the air and the many contemplative and meditative prayers being sent up. Here, there were no prayers, just an abnormal silence...and doors. Everywhere I turned there were more doors leading to the unknown.

There must have been three or four floors connected by multiple outdoor stairs situated throughout the building. Where did the stairs lead too? What happened behind each of the closed doors? Questions. I had so many questions fly through my mind within a matter of seconds. I wanted all the answers immediately. But no. I had to hold the weight of the unknown in my heart. The heat in my body intensified as I drew my own conclusions, and then I was guided to the other end of the compound.

I stood frozen in front of the last door at the very back of the building. I didn't know what I would find, but I knew it would be *something*. Immediately, the door opened and an endless line of women welcomed us and everyone who passed through the door. Their smiles did not reach their eyes. Their movements were monotonous...routine. I waited a moment as one of the women I came with spoke to someone. I felt like I was walking on needles. My legs were numb and goose bumps sprinkled the skin on my arms. My senses were heightened. I was soaking everything in and doing all I could to keep my fears and my thoughts in check as I stepped into and embraced—mind, body and soul—an experience that would shake every foundation I had ever stood on.

The room was dark. It seemed there was some sort of seating all around the room. It resembled a simplified auditorium...or a dark circus ring. No chairs, just the concrete floor molded into the shape of tall stairs. I found a seat alone—that was part of my training. Once we were in this communal area, everyone split up and I didn't know when I would see a familiar face again.

My heart was racing, pounding out of my chest. As my eyes adjusted to the darkness and my heart began to calm down in the quiet, I noticed a few others—maybe ten or so—sitting quietly throughout the room. I kept my head down mostly in fear of making eye contact with anyone sitting on the other side. I was being stretched inside in more ways than I could even imagine. I felt the tension.

My body wanted to run, but *I* wanted to know. I *needed* to see. I needed to see everything and take it all in. The Buddhists have a saying, "Unless you can feel it, taste it, smell it, see it, and hear it, it is not real." I didn't want to know by knowledge or learning—I wanted to experience it.

Our senses make things concrete for us. I was engulfed in my senses as I sat there waiting. Waiting for what? I did not know exactly. My palms were clammy and I wiped them on my jeans that covered my trembling knees. I was not sure how the night would play out, but I was far from home. I was far from anything familiar or comfortable.

After sitting for some time, a dim spotlight lit up a stage in the center of the room. One by one girls walked slowly onto the stage. They were thin, thick, short, tall... and all Asian. They were shy and timid. Some even seemed frightened. I did not know where to look. There was a lot of skin. It wasn't complete nudity, but I felt embarrassed and shy just seeing them. I felt extremely uncomfortable, and found my eyes drifting to my feet. My curiosity and desire to "know" compelled me to look back up. Slowly the girls began to dance. I found myself watching them move with barely anything on. I closed my eyes. I just could not watch.

My gut was doing summersaults, but I was there for a reason and I needed to find a way to focus. I decided to focus on their eyes. As I looked into the eyes of these young girls, I did everything I could to hold back my tears. The eyes speak so much and theirs were hollow. Most would not look at anyone.

Eventually, I just prayed.

I prayed that one would look at me, that one would *see* me. But then my mind raced...who was I? A small-town girl from Nebraska. What was I doing there? How could I make a difference? Could anything be done?

As I sat there, I noticed the men in the room. One motioned for a girl to come and she got down off the stage and joined him. Together they walked out of the area. The arena? The ring? I still had no idea what to call this place. More men came in and repeated the motions of the last—calling for the girls and escorting them away. They disappeared into the darkness. Would they be safe?

I was told that if one of the girls came up to me, I had the "okay" to engage in conversation and get to know her. We were also given some questions to ask, so that we had a general feel of her situation. I prayed again. I prayed so hard that one of the girls would come to me. Did women like myself—an observer—usually come to these types of places? Did the girls find it odd that women were there? The group of women I arrived with, we were the only females in the room...we sat quietly and expectantly. And we watched.

I hoped everyone was too preoccupied to notice us. I did not want to raise unwanted attention. We sat for an hour watching and waiting. My heart got heavier and heavier each moment that passed. These girls had no names, just faces and numbers.

The numbers hit me hard.

They were big, black and bold on a crisp white circle pinned to each of them. Sometimes the MC on the speaker (who I believe managed or owned the facility) would call a number on the loudspeaker and that girl would get down and be met by a complete stranger. He would be standing at the front door, then she would go off with him.

I did not know if I would be able to speak with anyone, but I desperately wanted to. I wanted so badly to meet one of them. I wanted to ask her questions and hear her story. Most importantly, I wanted to tell her she was important, to make her day, to bring something bright into her life. But could I? Did I have *anything* to offer? I wasn't even sure if I'd even get the chance.

The hour was *so* long. Seeing girls picked by their numbers and sent off like a product bought at a store was so devaluing. They were like cattle being herded, lined up, and given orders to. Yet all I kept pondering was the immeasurable value they each carried. They were people, someone's friend, someone's daughter, someone's sister or mother. They mattered to me.

The numbers screamed a different reality and they burned in my heart. They made me angry, sad, and I wanted to cry and vomit all at the same time. And then, number 107 looked at me and I looked at her.

This was the first set of eyes that found mine. She got down off the stage and came and sat right next to me. *Me*. In that moment all my fears, insecurities, anger, sadness, vanished. Who was this beautiful woman that sought me out that night?

I couldn't wait to ask.

I conversed for a meager ten minutes before the other ladies in my group left one at a time. I wanted more time. *Why? How?* There were so many questions swirling around in my mind and I felt like I was running out of time too quickly. I had been sitting in anticipation for so long, and now I finally had my chance...yet it seemed too short. But even in that short amount of time, it wasn't so much what we said to each other that I remember, it was that people matter. That simple truth will forever be imprinted on my heart.

I didn't hold back. My fears, my worries, my lack of knowledge about the issue, my uncertainty of the future...all of these seemed like such small inconveniences now. If people knew they mattered, and are of the greatest value, then we would be a force that no evil could stand against. This is the essence of love. Love knows no bounds and reaches all people—there are no strings attached, and there are certainly no numbers.

chapter two

Small Beginnings

I arrived in Thailand at the age of twenty-three with the faith, enthusiasm, excitement and zeal of a normal, young woman. Fresh out of University, I knew I was ready, willing, determined and eager to tackle some huge social issue. I just knew I could change the world.

I just wasn't sure *what* that social issue was...yet.

Having quit my job, I sold every possession I owned, packed what was left in two suitcases and I started out on my adventure. I was prepared for the "culture shock," or the different ways of doing things. I was expecting language barriers, but I was ready to create a new life. I felt that I could assimilate well. However, learning about it—mentally preparing for it— is *nothing* like living it.

Those first two years were filled with adventure, wonder and lots of firsts, but for me, the defining loneliness was a great burden to carry sometimes. I often refer to my first two years as "living in a silent bubble." I was living in a world where the only inhabitants were my husband and me. I felt isolated and alone.

For an extrovert, who was very active and high capacity—an American—my world had been rocked. For starters, my daily to-do list got shorter and shorter as time went on. Not being able to check off daily accomplishments was a huge blow to my ego and confidence. Eventually, celebration came the day I accomplished one to two tasks. Go shopping at the market, *check*. Figure out how to get hot water, *check*. I was elated.

Society operated on a completely different system than I was used to—one that was more event and relationship driven than time and task evaluated. Language was hard for me and I knew it would be. Thai is the fourth hardest language in the world, with five tones. *Five*. What is a tone? I still have a hard time pronouncing the words right. The pitches fall and rise like music; a melody with an undercurrent I only dream of mastering. One word can mean five different things depending on the tone it is spoken in. I hadn't imagined that not knowing the language would become so...detaching.

My husband, who had already lived in Thailand for five years, spoke fluently. I found myself tagging along with him entertaining myself with my own thoughts; as I couldn't understand or speak the language yet. These thoughts would eventually drift to my family, my friends and the life I had given up all in great hope of making a difference.

And yet, here I was years later, with barely enough knowledge of a language to order food and do the simplest tasks in the day, let alone, have a meaningful conversation with someone. I was at this time, friendless, weary, sad and defeated.

My best attempts at learning the language and assimilating into this new world failed. While sweating one night under the smoldering heat of the hot season, on the top floor of our apartment building, I tried desperately to fall asleep during another weekly power outage. The open window brought more noise than relief. While lying there miserably, I had an idea. This idea brought a flicker of hope to my weary soul and it was all I needed to convince myself to take action.

I needed meaning. I needed to feel *useful*. I needed something to do.

Life had become so hollow and depressing, so I began to research. Hours upon hours turned into days until I had my list of the top ten biggest issues currently faced in this new country that I had desperately believed I could somehow impact.

After downloading my finds to my husband, I shortened my list to the top three biggest problems and asked him if he knew anyone or any organization that focused on them. He was experienced in this culture and had many connections—whereas, I only had him.

He mentioned a few, and I narrowed them down to two options that tackled the top issues from my findings.

My excitement increased the moment I decided on my purpose. I could feel it rising, for me it came out boldly. I had a plan. I did not know the language, and I had no formal education in the task I was going to apply for, however, I had a phone number, a name and a location. I also had my list burning in my pocket. There was no Plan B.

Plan A involved volunteering. I offered my skills for the taking. Free. I wanted to help and serve in any way possible, even if it meant cleaning toilets or soiled bed linens. I knew if I could put myself in an environment where I could rub shoulders with and work alongside others inspiring change, it would bring meaning and joy back into my life.

I needed purpose, and I was about to find it.

My first option was volunteering at a home that took in individuals suffering from AIDS. It was usually their last home on earth. This home provided a comfortable, loving environment—a type of hospice service. My meeting with this organization got rescheduled, so I ended up visiting the next place on my list.

I found myself in a small, simple office at my second organization of choice. With a bit of reserve, I explained my lack of skills, but my willingness and passion to do anything. Their immediate response took me aback.

"Sure, you can join us. Most people who come on board do not last past two to three weeks. Our work load is very intense and emotionally heavy. There are people who *want* to do this...and then there are people who actually can. Trying it out is the only way you will know if you can handle this type of work load. What do you say?"

Umm. Yes.

I was floored! I had an opportunity! My excitement was contagious. I raced home to share the news with my husband, who was and still is my biggest fan, loudest cheerleader and strongest support. He champions me like no other.

I canceled my rescheduled meeting with the AIDS hospice and filled my mind with new found hope and excitement for the future. I had small flickers of faith. Faith that maybe I could make a difference, and hope that I would finally make an impact. The joy, not just excitement, but a deep fire rose within me. It engulfed me and my posture felt different, every breath I took tasted differently. I felt that maybe, just maybe, my life could have more meaning. *Could I actually be part of a team targeting top issues faced in Thailand?*

I could not wait. I tried to be calm and poised on the outside as I watched the clock slowly make its way around. I wanted to explode. This was me, all *me*. It was not me helping my husband, or tagging along on someone else's project. I was going alone and was paving my own path. Nothing felt so good and so right, and yet, I had not even experienced one day on the job.

It took forever for the night to arrive. I knew because I was counting each and every minute until my first assignment. My normal bedtime of 10:00 p.m. had passed. It was now 11:00 p.m. I kissed my husband, hopped on my motorbike and took off for work.

I felt the wind on my face and the movement of my hair on my neck. The temples with their omniscient presence towered high above. They cast an orange glow on the street below. I smelled the humid air and anticipation rose in me. I knew no fear. I had no worries. There were no emergency alarms disrupting the calm moment.

All I focused on in my thoughts was that I was going to get to meet people, learn about the culture more, and serve. Serve in some way that would help this land that still had not become my home.

I desperately needed this...and I hoped they needed me. How? I did not know, but I did not dwell on that. I was going and I didn't intend to hold back.

I turned my motorbike down a side alley and immediately my surroundings turned dark—everything looked and sounded different. Open air bars played loud disco music and sparsely dressed ladies lined the curb for a couple of blocks. I soaked it in, and then finally I had arrived.

The building was a modest shop nestled in the heart of our city's red light districts. I was anxious with excitement. The caution, the warnings...none of the fearful articles in today's world existed at that time. I was naïve of the real dangers I would be exposed too. Nothing was going to stop me from this.

I have had many people over the years ask me when I "found my calling," or tell me "you're lucky you know your calling." That term—found my calling—has always eluded me. My path had brought me to this point because first, I just wanted to know some of the biggest problems facing the country I was in. Secondly, I wanted to help create solutions.

It was really that simple. There was no divine voice, or moment, or even experience. It doesn't take a genius to see that our world has some huge and complex issues. I wanted to be a force of good and do something meaningful.

And in order for me to *do* something, I needed to step out and allow myself to have experience in sex trafficking...firsthand.

chapter three

STARTING OUT

A group of three of us departed and walked a few blocks. Yes, I was fully dressed. We stopped in front of an open air bar. Its blinking lit-up sign beckoned pedestrians to step in. One of the girls I went with knew the place well and asked to see someone specific. We were met with a small road block as the person we were looking for was not there that night.

In my zeal, I suggested trying a new place. My love for new places, new situations, and meeting new people overrode all of our fears. I took the lead and found another open aired bar with another obnoxiously blinding sign out front.

This place was sardined between a tiny row of shops. The darkness cast shadows as we walked in. A cat darted by, sending chills up my spine. The dirty concrete and cigarette burn marks led the way to the back of the shop. There were no windows inside and it looked empty—deserted, almost.

I passed a pool table first on the right side and two sets of wood trunk-shaped tables with matching benches lining the wall on the other side. Straight ahead, where my legs eventually led me, was a bar top and stools with the only exit a single door at the back wall.

There was a middle-aged woman working behind the bar, drying drinking glasses methodically, one at a time. She never looked up or even glanced our way, but continued to systematically perform her task.

On one stool a couple of feet away from me was another lady. She was much younger, engulfed in her phone that was covered in the popular Hello Kitty case. Her fingers were wrapped loosely around the device. Her long nails were freshly painted and sparkled with each movement as she texted back and forth with someone. Again, not once acknowledging anyone's existence.

I was this invisible profile walking around trying and hoping to capture someone's attention. In that moment, I felt insignificant and meaningless; always looking, but never looked at.

I could tell the other girls I came with were out of their element and I only imagined what they were thinking. It had been my idea to go somewhere new. I summoned up my courage and in my broken toneless Thai asked the women behind the bar what her name was.

Silence.

I tried again, this time a little louder. Both heads turned my way.

Finally.

She responded and I asked for a menu. The younger girl plastered to her phone found one for me while the older lady spouted off things far too fast for me to comprehend.

I quickly gestured for my team to take a seat. None of us spoke. Was it nerves? The adrenaline? Someone could have sliced right through the thick wall of fear between us girls. I figured I might as well do *something*, so I looked over the menu and focused on that other than my insecurities. I decided to order water.

To my surprise the menu was in English and Thai. Soon the young girl with her polished nails, twirling a pen, stood in front of us with an expectant look on her face. Surly, she wondered what else we wanted. We each ordered a drink and sat quietly.

When our drinks came I asked if the young girl wanted to sit down. She was surprised I asked—the shock was vividly written on her face. I imagined this had never happened to her before based on her reaction. She slid onto the bench across from me and I started speaking in the little Thai I knew. I asked what type of drink she liked. I bought her that drink. Soon her beverage was sitting on the table alongside our glasses of water. All my fears, all my doubts and all my own insecurities melted as we talked.

Her name was Kit. She knew some English and really wanted to learn, so we continued our conversation in broken English and broken Thai. She opened up more and more as the night went on. I knew that I wanted to spend more time with her outside of this evening.

We shared small talk mostly. She was from another city. She was twenty-one years old, had a brother and parents. She had graduated high school and started working at this bar one month ago. She loved animals and had a dog. I learned that her work hours were usually from 11:00 p.m. until the early morning. Kit told me she would get home at varying times and sleep most of the day, waking up around 5:00 p.m. to get ready for the following night.

She was beautiful to me, outwardly she had long silky black hair and did not have a traditional petite Asian body but more of a full shape and she was tall, at least my height of five foot seven. What I could not get enough of was her smile. Her eyes lit up when she talked, and she laughed so easily. She was bubbly, and fun, a classic enthusiastic cheerleader of sorts.

She motioned to another lady who arrived just then by motorbike. This one met up with us and pulled up a chair to join our conversation. I immediately bombarded her with questions. She was an older lady in her fifties and had two children in school. She was very shy, and quiet and spoke very little English. I empathized with her as we stumbled through language barriers and the obvious miscommunications that ensued.

Kit had to tend to a couple customers that came in and I found I was not able to get much information from O, the older lady. Soon I found myself at a loss of what to ask next. Feeling insignificant I found myself distracted by taking in my surroundings. The pool table and dart boards were prominent features that I noticed immediately. For the first time, I noticed a row of board games and card games lined neatly on a small ledge against the back wall.

I motioned to one of my teammates (who had sat there quietly the whole night observing and taking it all in) to grab a game. She brought back Jenga. Soon there was a refocus and concentration as we each tried to pull our wooden block out of the tower without it falling.

The air surrounding the evening wasn't as thick anymore. We weren't silent statues staring anymore. We were welcomed. As the game proceeded, my teammates began to warm up and started talking with O as well. I was enjoying myself but there had been an unspoken awareness.

I was still there to accomplish my mission.

I noticed every movement of Kit and the lady behind the bar. I watched an old guy struggle with his cane to sit atop of a stool. I watched him down one drink after another. I watched some younger men play a few rounds of pool laughing loudly and continuing to drink as the night progressed.

I observed all this while participating in Jenga at our table. One of the young men walked toward us to the bar and I saw something I had never seen in my entire life. To my horror and then utter shock, he had his crown jewels and manliness hanging out—waving it back and forth!

It happened so fast and he turned away from me but I could not believe it. Strangely, the night did not skip a beat, but continued on. No one blinked an eye. Thankful my teammates had not noticed, I tucked it into my memories to process at a later time. Preferably never.

The events of the night suddenly turned dark. It

was as if someone had flipped a light switch. Kit had to help the old man off the chair. He could barely stand alone or even walk for that matter. I watched as my new friend, kindly, gently and reassuringly held his arm and supported him as they walked to the back and disappeared behind the closed door.

I was experiencing firsthand things I had heard but did not really know. My heart was beating so fast. My instincts told me what was happening, but I needed more proof.

Armed with so many thoughts, I turned my attention to O in front of me, and started asking her about "customers." Every answer turned my stomach in knots. This bar was known as the "quickie bar." Yes, literally.

Usually the girls do not go off with someone but stay at the location. The going rate was ten dollars. I learned this was a great place for "newbie" girls, those who were starting out, ones with no experience. After they got their feet wet, they could move on to something better.

What types of experiences did they have to go through first? What criteria did they have to meet to move on? I couldn't think—didn't want to think—about how this quickie bar did business. My emotions and my mind could not keep up. All of my senses were heightened even as my head swam around in this fog of vagueness and uncertainty.

Soon a tuk tuk (an open air three-wheeled vehicle) drove up and stopped outside. A young girl stepped out with a sparkling cocktail length mini skirt and heels. It wasn't until she walked by me that I saw the bruises.

I wanted to help. I wanted to do something. What could I do? I was that invisible profile again. She had a black eye and dark marks on her arms. She looked like she had been crying.

As I watched, O must have noticed and shared that this bar was "safer." I didn't know what she meant by that.

"If you go away with someone, you never know what might happen...but the money is always better," she said. My heart broke. Maybe this was her...and my thoughts collided with O's next words, "first night on the job."

My world was being rocked and this girl had been violated. Helpless, alone, taken advantage of and *abused*. I sat there and watched as she gallantly walked through the threshold ready to begin her work shift. She looked defeated and yet she mustered the courage to continue.

Why? What's the reason?

I needed to know her story. I thought that maybe I

could help. That first night out left a lasting imprint on my heart. I had more questions than answers. I saw things I had never seen before. My faith and belief systems were tangled and my way of life had been completely shattered.

At home my husband was asleep in bed, and I was here doing research. Would *this* have been called research? One thing I knew for certain was I had made some beautiful new friends in the quickie bar.

I could not wait to come back.

chapter four

Lady Boys

As a newbie, my excitement was contagious. I loved going out at night. Meeting the ladies and hearing their stories was so fun to me. I would come home each night and debrief my husband for hours—usually a mix of my inner thoughts and emotions. I would find myself in tears of grief and sadness and then be smiling as I remembered how amazing it was to just meet and get to know someone new.

Every night I went out, my beliefs began to change because my experiences were so real and personal. Those people...labeled and known as a stereotype, shrouded in evil, violence and hopelessness, had become my friends—each with an actual name and an actual story. Once I had rubbed shoulders with someone different than me, I found that all my own stereotypes and judgments began to fall off like scales from my heart and mind. I could see their imminent beauty, the power they carried in just *being*.

I felt, in every fiber of my body, honored that I was given the opportunity to know them. I passed three weeks working with my team, like it was a long-lost hobby, something I loved to do dearly and yet just hadn't made the time for. The devastation and darkness around me couldn't keep me away.

I truly believe the depth of pain someone feels is directly proportionate to the love that person can feel. So, the immense heaviness and darkness that surrounded me when I went out in the evenings was equal in magnitude to the light I saw inside people. The beauty and strength I found stood firm, grounded and rooted in the mist of evil.

As an American who grew up in a sheltered, conservative, religious family I had been taught about the "evils" of homosexuality. Americans as a whole have many stereotypes and judgments of "those" people. However, as long as I can remember, I have never been repulsed by this. Instead, I am intrigued and curious.

In high school, I had a friend who came out. I remember it being very hard for him, but I also remember his courage and his pursuit to find himself. This was inspiring.

Thailand is on a different playing field when it comes to the LGBT community. Life threw me so many new curveballs on a daily basis that I would literally not be able to fabricate issues because I was surrounded by so much that was already challenging my beliefs, values and way of life—one being the issues surrounding the LGBT community.

One Sunday, while attending a western church in Thailand, I felt at immediate ease. It was as if an actual weight was lifted off of me. I was in a familiar place, a safe haven. I could connect to God in the way I was used to. It was comforting to participate in something familiar. I closed my eyes and lifted my hands, the best outward expression I could give for the gratefulness I felt.

When the music slowed down I opened my eyes and right in front of me, in the first row of the church, was a woman in a short, short skirt.

My first thoughts were "she shouldn't be sitting in the front seat," and "I wonder what her faith really looks like?"

My judgments caused me to notice her throughout the morning.

The next song selection was upbeat and very fast. As the song progressed I noticed this woman started to dance. This was not respectful especially with her choice of attire. In fact, I grew a bit angry and annoyed as this played out. As the song built to its crescendo, she spun around and I was hit with not a *she*, but a *he*!

What!

This is wrong, so wrong, on so many levels! Obviously, they have issues!

I felt offended that we were in a house of worship and this person didn't even have the audacity to show respect. How could this person have been worshiping God?

This experience brought my judgments to the surface, and then life in Thailand revisited these over and over. I was like an unwilling child, wanting my way...and day after day I was faced with a world that operated differently than mine.

In Thailand, bathrooms are merely facilities. They're never monitored and the signs are simply suggestions. I had become so used to looking up from washing my hands and seeing cross-dressers, or waiting in lines for the stalls to open smashed between a girl dressed like a boy holding hands with another girl and behind me stood a boy dressed like a girl. All these experiences that I had been engulfed in became my new norm and helped me rid my mind of the many judgments and stereotypes I unknowingly held.

If anyone ever suggested or even asked if I had any

judgments or prejudices against the LGBT community —or anyone for that matter—I would have been appalled. My best friend since the age of sixteen is a lesbian. This mere fact seemed to portray how inclusive and open minded I was. However, my inner thoughts when examined, and my immediate reactions, proved quite the opposite.

In America, the LGBT community is "fighting for their rights," and in Thailand they have equal if not more rights and opportunities. In Thai society, they are not defined by typical male and female roles. This allows them to pave their own way. For some, this is extremely beneficial. In Thailand one group known as "lady boys" are not cast-offs of society but an intricate part of it. It is the same even in the red light districts.

One night as I walked down the street, I made my way to a new bar front. It was a very lively night. A crowd of five to six western men were noisily playing pool and drinking, and a group of five to six Thai girls were laughing and smoking in a circle on the other side. I slid through the crowd without notice, found a seat and watched.

The ladies, I soon realized were kindly referred to as "lady boys." I was fascinated. I had so many questions to ask. Even though I had been exposed to so much, I hadn't yet met anyone that identified themselves in this way.

Friends change things. Friends draw out things inside of us. We listen. We create space inside our hearts for them. I wanted this with them. I mustered up the courage and motioned them over to my table. Some seemed shy and uncertain, but Om (the tallest) came over. She was extremely outgoing and we immediately started to chat. I ordered some drinks and settled into what had become an evening routine for me. Same mission, different bar.

Om talked so matter of factly. She had been born a boy. I was handed her driver's license and was shocked. I could not see any similarities to the beautiful lady standing in front of me and the small boy in the photo. There was even a different name printed on it. I found it interesting that Thailand accepted this license. The picture could have been someone completely different. Om was so comfortable with herself she did not feel like she *had* to get a new license. This city—this country— accommodates Om's identity regardless of if he's a "he," or a "she."

I got the impression there was no sense of shame or embarrassment attached to people knowing Om's before and after. She had a family and siblings and though she was young, seventeen, she aspired to get a complete sex change through surgery. Thailand is the leader in sex change surgeries.

I was again sent for a spin when Om's friend came over and joined us and her friend was *beautiful*. Absolutely stunning. I found it inspiring the amount of time the ladies took on themselves to look beautiful. The nails, the hair, the makeup. It was a bit loud and big for my taste, but the time, money and effort depicted something to me. This beautiful woman was born a man also. I don't think anyone would have been able to tell if one didn't know.

They began to discuss a pageant in Thailand for "lady boys." I was so intrigued when I got home that night I found the pageant on YouTube and watched it. Then I found the Miss Thailand pageant and watched that one, too. To my amazement, eventually I couldn't tell the difference between the "lady boy" and Miss Thailand winners! *Which one am I watching, again?*

Thinking back to the time I spent with those two brings a flutter of happy feelings to my heart. They were the friendliest and the most welcoming individuals I had met yet. I found it so hard to see them in a vulnerable place.

Their attitude and demeanor screamed passionately, "We are great, we are happy, we are living life fully."

I spent the next weeks getting to know them. We sat in a restaurant, and the restaurant was just a cover for a brothel—I knew what happened at establishments like these. I wasn't that same naïve girl anymore. I knew the workers there were exploited in some way. I knew my friends had struggles I was not aware of.

It was hard for me to weigh all that information with what I saw on the outside. I saw in myself the reality that I could see and yet choose not to see. What went on behind closed doors didn't seem as real as the image. This was alarming to me. If I hadn't known better, I could have convinced myself of an altogether different reality. Oh, how my culture and worldview shaped my assumptions and pre-disposition. My blindness in this area did not negate the truth of the issue. There is a worldwide epidemic and it's called modern-day slavery.

It is a darkness that prevails and it knows no gender. It hides in the shadows. It festers on the inside. It steals and kills value inside people. It entraps and enslaves. Boys are just as vulnerable too.

I did not want to embrace this. I had information and intellect, I even had some experience now. It had to change—I had to change, first. I needed to embrace my own ugly ideas and stereotypes hidden deep within. I needed to become aware. I decided to embark on that journey. I wanted to see change and I first needed to be that change.

I believe love sees. Love compels us to travel into the darkness so that we can create a path to the light. First it had to start in me.

chapter five

UNEDUCATED

I quickened my steps on this night. I stepped down off the curb so I could walk a path with less obstacles. I was in charge of picking a location. I knew exactly what I wanted to do: try something new...meet someone new. I was definitely the risk taker out of our group in this area.

The dangers were very real all around us and sometimes I would feel the weight of it in those moments of walking. It would fall on me like a blanket. It felt dark and heavy. I would normally push that feeling off and focus on *why*.

Why was I there and what could I do?

I have always been baffled by the reality that whenever one goes out of their way to help or show kindness to another human being, the return is priceless. I know the feeling after walking away from something—or someone—with more in my hands and heart than what I left behind. I wanted to give that to others.

As I continued down this path, I could feel and see the evident changes in my own life. While I knew what I was doing was small, the reward was life-changing. I sensed this so strongly, and the feeling amplified when I came home for my debriefing. *Can I do more? Am I really helping?* Those were the questions I repeated to myself. How does one move forward without knowing—truly knowing—the inner thoughts and lives of those affected in a system that takes away their dignity, measures them by a price tag and minimizes them to a number?

My focus was to learn. I did this with every part of my being—observation, sensing, questions, debates and debriefs. Why? I knew. My team knew. We knew that if we heard the stories, see and experience a bit of their lives, then we could create programs, homes, schools, job trainings and more based on what they wanted out of life. We could meet their needs where they needed help. The model was based on their own wants, desires and hopes.

I saw rampant hopelessness through the hollow eyes that would stare at me as I stared back. The eyes, void of emotion, void of sense. I experienced firsthand the effects of survival. The way it rolls around, gradually at first, like a snake encircling his prey.

I know how life can send you to the pit of hell yet doesn't disappear right away, it seeps out slowly. And before you know it, surviving has squeezed everything that was once alive inside you. Hope vanishes into the dark night. What is left is crumbs and remnants of a life you once knew...death has invaded.

Two ladies sitting on wooden bar stools motioned us across the street, thankful for the invitation we crossed the street. One of the ladies, Mink, and the other, Pi, began to express and share that they had seen us night after night for months walking down these streets. They wanted to know who we were and what we were doing. Something in my spirit leaped.

There are so many correlations to being present. Not only can you fully engage when you're in the moment, but any parent will tell you being present in your child's life is more valuable than anything money can buy. What a compliment we had just received.

As we talked a bit more, some ladies from inside the shop brought us some stools. We must have made for quite a sight, because the stares we got from by-passers were priceless. I was used to getting stared at in the bars by the clients and customers and some were even brave enough to speak with us. Most stares were either disbelief, questioning, or even directly put-offs. But this night we seemed to have made quite a unique impression.

People had to actually go down off the curb onto the street and walk around us—a mixed ethnic group of ladies chatting in a circle. I noticed this while also noticing that we were in front of a "massage parlor." I had never gone inside one (at that time) or met anyone who worked at one. This night, I was struck with the image of how exploitation takes on many shapes. Hidden in plain sight, unbeknown to most of those passing by.

I could sense Pi was not happy. Many of the ladies we had met, were great at keeping a face and acting. Only after countless evenings hanging out and building trust would we find answer to some of our questions and even get to more sensitive issues of the heart or even see the true desperation in their lives.

Pi was different. First, she was older, in her late fifties, she talked more openly, and was more inquisitive. My small talk questions turned to children and before Pi could answer, tears began to roll down her cheeks. Through the tears she told me about her two children, both teenagers.

As her tears ran faster, my heart beat faster. She began to share how they were at her home, sleeping for the night. They had no idea that she was gone. They did not know that she went out and "worked" in the night.

Months ago, her husband had abandoned her for another woman. She had found herself an uneducated woman, unable to find work and unable to pay for her children's school and put food on the table. One of her friends had suggested this type of work would pay good money and she didn't need an education.

My heart felt heavy.

She then proceeded to tell me the guilt and shame she felt. She began to weep. Pi shared through tears how the customers would come in looking for more than a massage.

I did all I could to hold back my tears, but they came out silently—one trickling down after the other running down to the tip of my nose and with a pause...then they dropped. The space that hung in the air seemed like it was suspended for an eternity, and then it hit the ground with such definition...like a period at the end of a sentence. It was inevitable. The reality of this moment felt like all I could do was reach my arm around my new friend and hold her tight.

Empathy was birthed. Sharing in one's pain created a bond in my heart like I had never experienced before. I could be there with her in this moment. When she had no more tears to cry, and through great anguish and internal struggle, she told me how she hated this type of work, and did not want to do it, but her children needed her. She shared how she never saw herself as *this*. She was harboring such shame, and could not even look me in the eyes. She dropped her head in overwhelming defeat and loss.

I could not rescue her from her situation, though I wanted to with every fiber in my being—it would not be sustainable. I was faced with this type of helpless, hopeless, dire emergency type situations daily. I reached for her hands. I positioned myself in front of her and asked her to look me in the eyes.

Out of the depth of my spirit came a sound. "You are not what you do. Your value and worth is immeasurable."

At that moment, I saw a lighted path in the darkness. This path was illuminated by love. We see its strength and beauty in mothers. A mothers' love does not back down, even when things oppose her. When obstacles stand in her path, her love knows no boundaries.

I witnessed this fierce love in Pi and the beauty of it challenged me.

How far would I go? How much do I love?

I had found myself connected more closely to humanity at 2:00 a.m. on a Thursday night sitting in front of a massage parlor, watching men walk in and out, stomping all over the women. Women who carried them not only in their womb but in their hearts. These are people who love fiercely, unconditionally...and yet they were treated as an object, something to be pleasured by, something with a price tag that can be bought.

There are many layers. I found that lifting one uncovers two or three more, and the deeper down I went...there were still more to uncover. The layers can feel depressing, just like the system.

One can be rescued, saved, restored—while at the same moment in time—another is taken, forced, or abandoned into the same wrath. Just the thought had me teetering on a tightrope straddling hopelessness and life. I didn't know if I wanted to take another step—a step with little foundation, a step slicing through the great darkness...

But I knew that this path was the path of love. I *needed* to.

Love is the antidote for our world's greatest problems. The solution. Love demands respect and value. That was what I brought each night. That is what the ladies felt. Love sliced through their darkness in those moments because my love demanded value and worth.

chapter six

Taken

One thing was consistent night after night as I made my way through the streets: the flickering brothel and bar lights casted their eerie glow over my path. I usually had some sort of interaction with a child. They were everywhere. Their dirty faces, dark hair and mismatched clothes all shouted the same message: poverty. They needed money.

Most of the ones that I had contact with were blunt. They would come up and tug at my clothes, begging for attention to give them some time and money. They either just wanted the money or they would try to sell me flowers for twenty-five cents.

I never saw a mother or father around but I was told many of them had parents working in the area—all of them were said to be uneducated and poor. These children were little. Their ages ranged from two to six years old.

I could always count on them to come around throughout the night begging and tugging on my clothes all while I was getting to know someone or sitting in a new bar. What I was amazed by, was how freely the ladies would give their money to these children.

In my years spent sitting inside bars, brothels and "massage parlors," I never saw one of the foreign (white) male customers give. The children who tried would walk away empty handed every single time.

My heart would break each time I would interact with one of these children. I struggled immensely with helping in this way. I saw firsthand that once one of my teammates gave regularly, those children would swarm in aggressive packs, begging for more the next night. It seemed to intensify with each coin.

It felt dangerous. It was ravenous and overwhelming. It felt like a battle that could not be won. And was it effective? Yes. Perhaps it gave them food for the night, but did it actually perpetuate the cycle? What were they supposed to do? I definitely was not angry at the ones who gave and I never told someone *not* to give. I wanted to do something more...but what?

On this particular night, while sitting in a bar—the usual—I was half-heartedly engaged in a conversation, but internally studied the people passing by. Suddenly, all my alarms were going off in my head and getting louder and louder as I observed a scene unfold across the street.

A group of six little children were gathered, playing and talking together, and I saw a white man walk up to them and say something. The children in their habitual routine tried to sell him some flowers and extend their hands for some coins...all to no avail. This man turned around and left. I did not think anything of it until a few moments later. He returned.

Bending over he positioned himself eye level with them. I wasn't sure what he was doing or saying. All I knew was he left the children empty-handed again. I continued to watch. As he turned around to head back down the street for a second time, one of the little boys was with him. He was grasping the little boy's hand and walked back down the road from where he came. The boy was not struggling and did not seem in distress, but I was. What was going on?

I stood up out of my chair, my heart raced and my thoughts pounded. I did not want to make a scene, I did not know if anything bad was taking place, yet something did not seem right. My motherly instincts must have connected, because every part of me said that whoever that little boy was, *he mattered.*

I truly believe the power of love invaded every part of me and I could not sit back. I had to do something...I watched and my mind raced. *What should I do?* As I watched the man and boy hand in hand continue down the street fading in the distance, I decided to follow them.

I kept myself at a safe distance. I did not want to cause a scene. I did not want the little boy's safety to be at risk. I continued down the road not wanting them to get too far ahead. I needed to be close enough to do something, but far enough not to raise suspicion.

The man picked up some speed and I continued faster, faster and faster. As the man began to cross the street, I saw it—an empty tuk tuk waiting. I picked up my pace a bit more. I had no plan. I had no idea where my team was. I had one thing on my mind: the safety of that little boy.

As if on cue of my arrival, the man let go of the little boy's hand and turned to the tuk tuk driver to give directions. At that moment, I grabbed the little boys hand, walked a few steps down the road and sat him down on the curb with me. He was no more than four years old and seemingly unfazed by what was happening.

It was then that I noticed my team around me. They were like a shield of protection and comfort in a sea of evil. I tried to regain myself. I sucked in breath after breath as if the life of me had been squeezed out. And as I breathed, I looked around and down the street in the direction from where I had sat just moments ago. In bar after bar, shop ladies were standing and shouting in Thai. It was as if I had enlisted a team that night.

I tried to talk to the little boy. He would not talk, he just sat there. We did not know where his mom was or where he should go. One of my teammates gave him a few coins and he jumped up and ran off. I however, could not think let alone move. I don't remember how I got home, only I somehow managed to and then I collapsed into a heap of tears. I wept for hours.

I did not feel any excitement or gratefulness of my heroic rescue that night. Did I stop something that could have ended tragically? Yes, but I could not however stop thinking...what about tomorrow? What about all the other children roaming the streets after dark? It was so easy for someone...it made my skin curl and my body sweat. I could not rescue everyone. Was I doing enough?

I was so tormented by this scenario. It would have been easy for me to quit. Quit going out, quit meeting the girls, stop trying to help, quit putting myself in such dangerous and evil environments. The internal struggle was hard to work through each night, let alone the physical environment.

This was why when I first joined this organization, they said most won't stay on after three weeks, and the average worker stays for only six months. I can testify that when one is surrounded by a completely different world then you're used to operating in, your belief about everything—how you live, your money, your family, your job—get questioned and turned upside down. Not only are you navigating things you have never experienced for the first time, which is a very vulnerable and scary place to be, but everything your life was grounded on gets put on the questioning block to be interrogated.

The fear was so real for me. It felt as if everything on the inside was exposed. I found myself battling the thoughts of hating myself and my entitlement, my attitudes and judgments...and then I began questioning my worth, my lifestyle of comfort versus theirs of poverty and risk. I was no better than them, yet I was born in privilege by comparison.

I was so impacted by this...I couldn't stay away. Those people in the dangerous, unsafe part of town had become my friends. I could not abandon them. I might not have much, but I was loyal and I could walk with them. This I knew. So, the next time I went out, I planned to meet with one of my friends at the bar first, and then spend half the night with the street kids. I filled a bag with treats, coloring books and crayons.

Those corners became filled with coloring and playing games. I desperately hoped I could keep them all out of harm's way for the night. I hoped I could build trust. I wanted them to know if anything did go wrong, that I would be there to help. I hoped that their parents would check them into our after hours childcare—a safe facility located on the same street. A place full of love and hope.

However, many of those children were on the street because their parents needed them to be. The family needed the extra money. It saddened me each night I interacted with them. I knew their little bellies were hungry. I could never image my four and six-year-old sons begging for money on the side of the street.

I panic at the thought.

It also makes me want to adopt every child in need. The harsh reality these families face leaves their children vulnerable. Survival is such a nasty thing. It takes away hopes and dreams. It is unsafe and risky. It steals futures. From that moment on, I decided to get to know these children by name. They would not stay invisible. They would become known and cared for and loved.

chapter seven

BAR FIGHTS

My friend was there ready for the night activities, fitted in her tight short little black dress. I was always amazed anyone could walk in the five—or maybe six—inch heels that she wore. The sidewalks, roads and curbs were so uneven. My own attempt at heels in Thailand left me with a sprained ankle one time.

I had started spending extra time getting ready in the evenings. Maybe my own self value grew through this experience. Maybe I was just inspired by my new friends. They always looked so put together and they would take hours to get ready. I felt challenged to do the same.

I had hated the fact that our team had voted to wear matching shirts representing our organization. We worked with their logo blasted on the front of our T-shirts. I imagine it came from cultural customs. Every school and job in Thailand (no matter the age) has a uniform. I think they believed wearing our logo would help with team dynamics and also show others who we were and what we were doing there.

My Thai teammates also struggled with unwanted stares and assumptions that they were connected to the system when they would go out each night. They had to take on judgments and the stress from their family and friends who are part of a belief system within Buddhism. Many followers in Buddhism do not want to be associated with bad Karma because it will inevitably rub off onto them.

It is also believed in a future life, one could be demoted to the very thing that was "rubbed off" onto you. My teammates would get disapproval, scorn and even be treated less than and lower than others by their family members and peers—just for helping those working in brothels and go-go dance bars. Wearing the T-shirts may have come from the idea of wanting to show that we were different and not one of "them."

The immense battles that we faced individually and as a team were ones that were not talked about, but ones that we lived with daily. I was not opposed to anything. I understood the different sides and their perspectives, however, I observed the reactions of those we were trying to reach and then I adjusted.

I found these "rules" to be off-putting and to me they seemed to have the opposite effect than what was hoped for or intended. Wearing matching clothes and going together in a group of three to five was odd. We stood out and in my opinion not in a good way. We were not very approachable. We were already different, but now we were *really* different.

I found it difficult to blend in on the streets and come and go with ease. We would get stopped by a lot of the male customers that spoke English and would question us on what we were doing and why we thought we could actually do something. They usually tried to convince us that this is a free world and people are here by free choice.

I found these conversations all a massive detour in our focus and our goals. So, I did not wear the uniform and tried to split the group so it would only be two to three of us in a location at once.

Dressed to impress, I hit the night with a pep to my step. Rumors must have spread, because the night talk turned to children. The ladies at the bars began to tell me stories—things they witnessed, fights that broke out and kids that had been taken.

They opened up to me like never before, and there seemed to be a shift in the atmosphere. I felt like I belonged, that they embraced me. Somehow, they knew I didn't care about what they did—I cared about them.

A very well dressed businessman in his fifties pulled up to our bar that night in a tuk tuk. On his arm was a Thai girl wrapped in a white fir shrug. This seemed a bit of an odd dress choice with the weather being so hot (at least 100 °F on this night). I quickly determined in my mind that it may have been a gift, or maybe the man liked that or maybe it was her most prized and expensive article of clothing.

Whatever it may have been didn't really matter. I was jolted out of my thoughts by a huge argument that had broken out literally a few feet in front of me between these two. It kept on escalating, and the next thing I knew the girl was swinging her purse and the guy threw a punch, knocking her off her feet and onto the hard pavement. In that instant, a flood of bar girls came out from every bar down the street (it seemed) and started yelling and cursing.

Then the lady boys jumped in and held off the man from doing any more damage. The manager of my bar stepped in, and in her broken English demanded the man leave. She did this all while standing in front of the girl on the ground—like a shield. It was a beautiful picture.

The man was drunk and had a very hard time walking down the street. As he went off, the girls helped pick up and shoulder the girl who had been attacked, taking her into a back room. Everyone dispersed back to where they each had come, and then it was quiet. I was stunned into silence.

It happened so fast. It didn't seem there was much I could do. I just witnessed everyone on the street rallying together against someone who was "not one of them." But, as I tried to sort my thoughts out, that man came wobbling back.

This time, he did not come to our side of the street but to the side where the children were. I shot up out of my seat faster than my mind could formulate a plan. This was *not* happening again. He was drunk, violent and not in his right mind. As I rushed out across the street I was joined by a couple of other bar girls. They ended up stepping up before I could and managed to calm the man down and guide him into a tuk tuk that drove him away. I couldn't believe it.

As I slowly walked back, I couldn't help but return the smiles and nods that I was getting from ladies standing on watch in front of their bars. They had joined me in my cause. They did not know those kids, yet they knew the risk and tragedy those children faced.

Somehow my actions the other night had paved a tangible way we could all join together in. I couldn't help but feel empowered.

Life matters, people matter and love fights for a brighter future.

chapter eight

AIDS

On this night, while walking, we decided to take a quick stop at the local 7/11. It was like a gas station shop without the gas. 7/11's are everywhere in Thailand and they are a really convenient place to grab a snack or refreshing beverage, which was on my mind this hot, steamy night.

Even before entering the convenience store we were bombarded by street children wanting money and selling flowers. One of my teammates couldn't resist and started handing out coins one by one. I used the distraction to duck into the shop. Once inside I hurried to the back, grabbed a cold water bottle from the fridge, and headed back up to the front to pay.

Having finished up my purchase before my teammates, I headed outside to get away from the crowd and the long line that was engulfing the tiny shop.

While outside I sat down on a curb, cracked open my water, started sipping, and watched.

People watching is a very intriguing time filler.

While I was sitting there I noticed the dirty children hopping from one person to another—begging. I saw the ladies, the ones who did not have a customer yet, standing outside their bars. Some were dancing, some chatting with each other. Motorbikes whizzed by down the street and an occasional tuk tuk weaved through as well.

There was some sort of Thai disco music blaring, and muffled under that was a song playing in English. I imagined it had to be one of the top radio songs, but I didn't really know. Having lived in Thailand for three years at this point, I was not up-to-date on the current artists and music. However, I had been hearing the tune of this song for a few weeks now.

I kept watching.

The always consistent food carts were parked on the side of the road and I watched as the women working in prostitution, the managers, the pimps, the lady boys, the children, the foreigners, and the customers would purchase something from the same cart and walk away. The farang (white) customers dotted the street. They were very easy to identify. They towered over everyone, making them an easy eye target, and their white skin stood out in a sea of brown.

As I watched, I saw a small person walking toward me. He—or she—walked with a limp in a slow deliberate way. Their eyes were covered by a dark hood and their hands were pushed deep into pockets on the front. Their head was bent down as they walked. I saw them stand outside the 7/11 trying to get the attention of a few people walking out, but the people would glance and continue on in the opposite direction. I didn't know what they needed or what they said, however, I could tell that this person was poor by the dirty, three sizes too big hoody and tattered shorts. The feet were the final convincer for me. Most Thai wore sandals. Those in extreme poverty usually had really dirty feet. This person's feet were *so* dirty it was as if they hadn't bathed in months.

As I watched, my attention followed the sound of a very loud engine roaring to a start. Soon a streak of color sped by. It was one of those beautiful Kawasaki racing bikes. It's pure sleekness and speed would leave me dreaming about riding one...and my thoughts wandered down another trail yet again.

I turned and was brought back to reality. That person I had observed just a moment ago was now sitting next to me on the curb. The movement I made to look toward them must have given them the courage they needed to speak. Soon I was talking in Thai to a very timid, yet desperate girl.

It felt as if her eyes were searching mine, uncovering something inside of me...her desperation felt like a load of bricks keeping me glued to my seat. As I listened, my thoughts swirled. Maybe it was the fact that she was my age, and had resorted to begging strangers for money. My life seemed to flash before me. She persisted, not harshly or loudly, but in her quiet way. Her demeanor carried hopelessness. As she talked, her words gained strength and conviction. She needed money desperately. She didn't want any food, she needed medicine.

I was completely enthralled in my conversation with this girl. Everything else around me—the noise of the people, the ring of a bell whenever someone would come in or out of the of the 7/11 door behind me—faded into oblivion. In that moment, it was just her and me. What was I going to do?

Normally I didn't hand out money, but I was compelled by her story so I dug in and questioned her. "Medicine?"

She then lifted her sleeves, bearing her arms. My heart sank...my body tensed and my mind went into overdrive. Sores! Open oozing sores. I had never seen sores like that up close, especially not in this part of town where the ladies were presenting their best image night after night. Just as quickly as she had lifted her sleeves, she pushed them back down and continued with her story. Why was she in this area of town? All this time, I was taking her words in one at a time, like a precious gift I had just been given. I remember feeling that this experience would become a foundation for me.

Those sores were advanced signs of AIDS. I had known this was a huge issue in Thailand, but to see it so raw and in the flesh made it real. She was in pain, and yet I couldn't possibly fathom her next words.

The medicine she needed was for someone else.

Wait, what?

I was ready to help her in any way I could by this point. I could tell her pain was real as she winced any time she moved. I imagined some of the pain was brought on by the rubbing of her clothes on those open wounds.

I found out she had a boyfriend who was waiting for her. She was his sole caregiver and provider...he was dying. With tears in her eyes she wanted the medicine for him because he was in so much pain. She knew his pain intimately. He was dying a slow death from AIDS as well. My breath was taken from me, but how could

I *really* help? I mean really...money for medicine, yes...but here I was literally facing death...talking to death.

I had experienced death in a very real way once. I was a teenager. My best friend who lived in the house next door to me was murdered. The feeling of that night when I came home and saw bright lights and yellow tape...it will forever be etched in my memories. But this was different.

I was experiencing death from another angle. Death has the final say when the last breath slowly ceases. Yet its strong grip on us, while we are alive, can feel so incredibly unbearable. The sheer act of surviving sucks the breath out of us. I felt engulfed in this force in the form of this woman I had just met. Her story was not finished. She had more to tell. I was already having a hard time as I was continually connecting dots and experiences in my own life. She courageously persisted on. There was a baby. She had a baby...and the baby was born with AIDS.

Sometimes the world seems too cruel, so hard, unfair, and dark. My problems were nothing compared to the real needs and desperate survival of her family. I was in the right place at the right time. That moment in time painted the clearest picture of modern-day slavery

I have ever witnessed. To this day, I hold that moment in my heart as such a priceless gift.

Together, my team and I decided to pool all the money we had that night, which wasn't much, and help. Two of us went back into the 7/11 to grab a pack of diapers and some formula, while the other girls stayed and talked with my new friend. With our arms loaded we exited the shop.

I had been exposed to hard situations many times, and I worried a lot over what was the right thing to do. This was one of those times. I watched my friend hobble away with a load too heavy.

Are we doing the right thing, sending her away like that? Should we go with her?

Experience had taught me that even if you ask for contact information, or genuinely offer for them to call you, or get in touch with you, rarely is this reliable. The chance of me seeing her again was slim to none. The reality was that the number she would give could possibly not work, or was not legitimate. Maybe the address belonged to someone else.

My mind bounced from one experience to the next getting more down on myself as I walked away. It was never safe to go back with someone. This was not only part of our organization's rules, but it is a safety standard that I would teach to new volunteers...and yet I was so unsettled.

For days afterward, I could not get this encounter out of my mind. This experience connected dots in ways I had only heard and read about. For me it was so powerful and life gripping. I kept going back to what I had witnessed, the cycle.

The reason she was walking on that street begging for money was because she used to work on that street. She had been one of the bar girls. I couldn't get the vivid picture out of my mind. She had been one of the beautiful girls dressed to impress with nails, hair, and makeup.

The smiles, the fun times, the outgoing personalities. It was a façade they learned by force or through being indoctrinated to show the world. The shots, one after another, that helped them survive, that numbed the gnawing feeling of hopelessness and worthlessness. The business of late nights and lack of sleep that kept them from thinking about the struggle, the pain, the trapped feelings. What a stranger could see from the outside was a mere surge that with even a tiny puncture would erupt into Niagara Falls.

It doesn't take much except time, awareness, and care to see that everything is not okay. I saw this firsthand, the hell of their lives. The fears and vulnerabilities they faced daily. She had been one of them...and all it took was one night with someone. Now she was dying.

She was dying a slow painful death. Barely surviving. Begging. The ugliness infected her entire family. To make it worse, there was a second generation born into its cruel grasp. Her value was taken, stolen. She was literally left on the shelf to rot. Left to die alone.

The cycle of modern-day slavery is crushing. It shows no mercy. It gains strength through supply and demand.

I saw the full circle of reality for every one of my friends...a lonely, painful, suffering existence. These thoughts were like knives that pierced me. Sometimes the intense pain I would get from reliving the moment and going deeper into the parallels would leave me bent over in agony. This is life...this is life for them...this was the clearest picture I had ever seen. It was hard for me to bear. I couldn't, I had to do more. I continued to challenge myself to change.

Thankfully, we were able to find another non-profit that was a type of hospice that cared for those dying of AIDS. They allowed each person to rest and die in peace. We were also able to find another non-profit organization (NGO) that was for moms and babies. They took my friend and her baby in.

The memories are vivid and they live inside of me every day. The feelings that overcome me, even to this day, are a constant reminder that love wins. Love is a force that can be so violent, it shakes every thought and belief inside your core...it propels you to see value and takes note of needs...love is the selfless act of stepping outside of your comfort zone so that you can be in the right place at the right time.

I am so fortunate to have grown up in a family that loves me, values me, and cares for me. I can pass this on to someone who has never experienced that. You cannot give what you have never had.

I never realized how much of my life I took for granted. I somehow intrinsically believed that every person had this. Love is this force, sometimes vicious in its pursuit, but it is always constant in one thing: the worth of a person. You are enough. They are enough. When you see this, or when you feel this, take note...love is there.

chapter nine

THE SYSTEM

Every society trafficks in some sort of hierarchy. Some look more racial, some political, or some financial. Some are more blatant and up front, and in some cultures, it's not talked about but rather a code or system of operation. It permeates most societies and cultures. It is a hidden, unspoken "rule." This is also the case in regard to sex trafficking and the system within the red light districts. I found myself completely shocked that there was some sort of system like this.

I remember sitting with Ann one night at a bar. In a conversation, she told me that she had worked herself up in the bars. At that time I did not really know what she meant by that. Over the next few months I began to get a clearer picture.

I found out through many conversations with many different girls that there were bar levels. I learned that each bar that the girls worked at was situated on a hierarchy. It was like an organizational chart at typical office jobs. The lowest bar on the list did not allow the girls who worked there much choice. "Much choice" can be an entirely separate book—none of the girls came into the business by choice. However, in their own perspective within their situation, their everyday life could get better. It is from this thought that I learned of the choice and options they had.

So much of what I learned took time. It was hard to rush to conclusions when I only had pieces of the puzzle. Some of the hardest moments I endured involved sitting and watching. Not being able to take action tore at my insides. Many months went by and I continued to put different pieces of the puzzle together, all in my attempts to get a clearer picture of their reality.

The girls working in the lower bars had to stay there. They were told with whom and where to go and usually did not make very much money, if any. Sometimes, if they tried to run away or leave without permission they would get locked up and pressured into submission by force. It was also this bottom level that did most of the recruiting.

Many times, the managers and the bar

owners were the pimps. They would usually be the ones responsible for getting the girls to "work" in some type of way. However, figuring out who these pimps *were* was challenging. Their looks were so deceiving.

I remember getting to know one manager, Pim. She was a short, older lady—maybe sixty something years old. She had silver stripes through her hair and a soothing, calming voice. Pim worked the back bar and I would chat with her here and there whenever I would come in. I found her very endearing. She would look after the girls and had a kindness in her voice. I had the sense she was like a mother and grandmother figure to many. Unbeknownst to me at the time, Pim was the main person responsible for recruiting the majority of the girls on that entire block.

It was at another bar, meeting and talking with two other girls, that I started to put more pieces of this story together in my mind. One of the girls, Ming, was shy and timid. She didn't talk much, but was very kind and smiled often. She usually sat with the other girl, Pie, each night. I sensed that Pie comforted Ming.

Pie was chatty. In one of our conversations she shared how she recruited Ming to work with her. I couldn't believe it. Why would someone do that? Ming seemed grateful for Pie's efforts. When a customer would walk in, Pie would reassure Ming and then turn to me and with a shrug and say, "She will get used to it."

I felt sad. I didn't know what I could do in moments like this.

I learned through Ming that the manager would send her—or one of the "trusted" girls—back to small villages throughout Thailand and recruit girls for jobs. Ming shared with me how Pim recruited her. Pim told Ming that she had a restaurant and bar that paid good money...that she would take care of her and that she would be safe. I remember asking Ming if she knew the "other work" this job required.

Ming looked at me with hollow eyes and shook her head. I sensed she felt a sort of betrayal.

In each conversation I had with different girls at different bars, none of them knew the type of work they would be getting into when they were being recruited. I was amazed to find most girls had such a loyalty to Pim even though to me it seemed she had lied and tricked them into coming. The way the girls explained it to me, it appeared Pim kept her promise and the girls got paid.

Ming finished our conversation by sharing with pride how much freedom she had now. She had been working for Pim for one year and life was better. She was not working at the lower bar anymore but was now working at this new bar.

The new bar allowed the girls to come and go. They could choose which customers they wanted to go with and where. The pay was much better. This meant better clothes, nicer shoes and better living quarters. Ultimately, I saw that the more control someone had over another person, the more violated that person was.

It is the complete opposite of love. Love says the more freedom of choice one has, the more love one will find, see, and feel.

So in a small way I began to see the bar system in light of more freedom of choice for the girls. With that thought I sensed there was love. I was able to rejoice with my friends when they would "advance." I could see the little bit of extra freedom they felt.

The newbies had it rough. I could always tell who was new. The fear and their attempt to distance themselves to customers when they would come in would give it away. These girls started out at the bottom.

The new girls were the lowest possessors of a system that sold sexual pleasure—a system that *still* sells sexual pleasure.

These first-timers started their work by getting "broken in." You see, once a girl knows she can't get away, or has accepted the situation, her mission changes. She throws her efforts and focus into moving up or advancing. She wants to create something better for herself. Possibly bring a better life than the one she unexpectedly found herself in.

I find we all do this. It must be an essential component in humankind. The need to grow, to move, to achieve, conquer, and survive. Within the darkest places in the world, survival is at an all-time high, a necessity, a drive. That drive pounds down on, runs over and tramples anything in its way.

I felt this survival in two ways: I was so empathetic to the plight of the girls and for their freedom and choice. My soul longed for them to see that they were valuable. I wanted them to see it for themselves too. There was the other side of the coin too...this was the ugly elephant in the room. The ugly side of survival. It was hard for me to even embrace it. I really just wanted to throw it aside and not deal with the ugliness. It was huge and invaded my thoughts. I decided to tackle the mess head-on. So began my attempt at navigating the ugly side of survival.

Hurting people hurt people. This has never been more true or vivid than in the pit where people are treated as commodities. A space that thrives on vulnerability and feeds off it. Exposes the pain, exploits the weak and takes everything. This place is survival.

Night after night I saw firsthand the ugly side of survival where people found ways to move up in a system founded on deception and pain.

Inside this system were rules. Only the best, most creative, and brilliant would win. One could look at it as a "game" that needs to be played or beat. I witnessed firsthand how this looked with a girl that I met one night.

One of the girls I had been visiting for months had really opened up with me. We had enjoyed many nights getting to know each other and sharing small bits of our lives. As time progressed, these small bits became more personal. I loved hanging out with Oy. She was soft-spoken, calm, and was up to do just about anything.

I was pleasantly surprised when I got a phone call from her. I probably would have done anything she asked. In my first year of going to bars, I had collected phone number after phone number of the ladies I had met and continued to see. Each time I received a new number I would practically beg them to call me. I would do my best to convince them that I was available at any time if they needed me. In all that time, I had never gotten one call...and Oy changed that.

After composing my ecstatic emotions, I answered

the call. My mind raced. It was early afternoon and usually the girls working at the bars were sleeping at this time. I immediately thought something must have happened and my heart started pounding and my body braced itself for the impact.

"Want to come over to my house and do nails together?" Oy asked.

I couldn't believe it. No help, no emergency, just a "let's hang out." I said something calmly and got all the details. I scribbled on my paper the time and location. Inside, my heart was jumping. I felt like a seven-year-old school girl going to get ice cream! I grabbed my keys and hopped in my car.

I arrived at an apartment building three blocks from the bar Oy worked at. It took me forever to find parking.

Many of the old city areas were not built for modern cars and the heavy traffic. Sometimes it is nearly impossible to find a place for a car to park. I circled three times. I was not going to miss this opportunity because I could not find a lousy parking spot. I decided to say a quick prayer in hopes of a miracle. As I slowly circled again, I noticed my friend standing on the curb waving at me. I pulled up. She then informed me there was underground parking at her building.

Hooray!

Once parked, I met up with her on the ground level and she guided me through the labyrinth of floors. We began the steep trek, taking each outdoor staircase upward. As I walked up eight flights of stairs, I tried to calm the nervous excitement I felt. I looked over the balcony and took in the streets, the temple off to the side, the smells of Thailand... I breathed. At that moment, life was good. I was happy.

Once inside her place, I made myself comfortable on her bed. I gazed around the small studio room. There stood a small college size fridge in one corner and a desk next to it. I sat on a king-sized bed, that took up ninety percent of her room. There was a small bathroom, completely tiled with the traditional squatty potty on the ground and a shower head hanging above it.

In many Asian countries, the entire bathroom is the shower. This means that nothing can be left in the bathroom or it will end up wet.

She really adored stuffed animals, it seemed. They were everywhere—except the bathroom, of course. They covered every available surface. The bed was full of them. Small ones and huge ones. She even had a white bear bigger than me. There had to have been over one hundred stuffed animals.

She also had another collection of random knickknacks. This collection ranged from dried flowers to ceramic figures in plastic. All these little trinkets engulfed and took over every inch of her tiny space. I assume she kept every single thing she was ever given. Her room was literally a shrine of her entire life. The people who had come and maybe gone.

Oy dug into a pile of soft animals. Emerging, she produced a tall towering plastic tub. The tub was filled with nail products. Oy was a nail tech. I had never known this. I found out she went to beauty school and acquired her certificate in it. She would do it on the side for her friends for extra money.

She had everything, glitter, stones, acrylic. I was in for a treat. As she did my nails, we talked. When I talk, my whole self is engaged. My hands move. My body is responding. My senses are all turned on.

People matter to me. They are of highest worth and greatest value in this world. My world, that involves lots of to-do lists, challenges, and struggles, easily disappear —like rain washing away mud—when I am with someone. People energize and bring a focused flow to me.

That was how Oy made me feel.

I was fascinated with Oy and her story. She started her story at a time when she had been doing nails at a shop close by. Her friend had stopped by and asked if she wanted to make more money. She was interested in that. Without knowing any details, she agreed to meet her friend that night and learn more.

That very night, her friend introduced her to a complete stranger. This man was from Europe. As I listened to her story, I was again overcome with how prevalent this scenario played out. Here I was, again, hearing it.

I was in another place with another girl. I interrupted Oy, wondering how she felt, being introduced to the man. I never found out how she felt. She did not want to stay on that part of the topic for long—I didn't blame her. She brushed the comment away and went on to the next part. The best part. The exciting part: money.

More money than she had ever made before and in such a short time. With her nail job, she would have to work three to four full days to earn that much money.

Her friend found her another customer the next night. After some time and steady income, Oy quit her job at the nail salon. She began working at a bar with her friend. This is where I had met her. The money was good, really good for Oy.

She shared how sometimes things would get complicated for her. Once, a customer had gotten really mad at her when together they had come across a customer Oy had been with a few days earlier. One time Oy said they actually got in a fist fight and she had to call the police, who got involved. I could not imagine. My life looked so different. I listened on.

Oy did not like that kind of drama. She needed the money, not the complications. So she started to share with me how she would keep her "men" in order. I was baffled.

Men...in order?

What did that mean?

To my growing surprise, she began to share details about all of these men—what they would give her, financially and also materialistically. As I sat there dumb-founded, I felt I was being taught by some sort of mastermind. She was a sales genius.

Sales reps sometimes get the tough end of a deal. There is the skill of communication and also the feeling of manipulation all rolled up into one. Sometimes it can be hard to navigate the intentions of the person. I could not help remembering a conversation I had at a local bookstore. The owner pointed out that his shop along with most other bookshops in Thailand carried the same two types of books. These two book genres compiled the majority of the bookstore. The first book type he labeled "My time in Thai prison." These were accounts of foreigners who had spent time in jail.

The second book type he labeled "How my Thai girlfriend took all of my money." These were accounts of men who had been swindled of every penny they owned. I was shocked that there were hundreds of accounts of these. I couldn't help but feel, as I listened to her story, that Oy could probably fit into the second book stereotype.

Some of the men would take her on trips and pay for everything. She listed at least ten places she had visited. Most of the locations were high-end resorts and beaches. My friend, a simple nail technician from a small village, worked at a bar in one of the red light districts and was living a high life. She brought in over $2,000 US a month through her many customers. I could hear in her voice how proud she was. Proud of her experiences. Proud of the life she was making.

I couldn't believe it. Her story was uncommon in many ways and yet similar in others. Part of me wanted to celebrate with her and the other part of me sensed some type of reserve. My mind raced to process but still stay in the moment for her.

Soon I got confused. *Really* confused. She would use past tense and present pronouns interchangeably. When she would speak about the men she had been with and the guys she was with now, they seemed to overlap in some weird way. I knew she was with many guys at once—customers. I was, however, unclear of what she meant when she kept referring to them as her boyfriends. How could one person possibly have that many boyfriends at one time? My idea of a boyfriend was clearly different than her idea of one.

I thought maybe I was missing something. That somehow, something was getting lost in translation. Sorting out the meanings of things was challenging with her broken English.

Some of the men seemed to be one night stands or just cold calls. Other men seemed to be more. I found it hard to navigate the depth of the different relationships she had. I also found it confusing to understand who was a past relationship and who was a current relationship.

Were they all paying customers or were some of them...lovers? I had a hard time wrapping my mind around what she was saying and the very thought of what she was implying.

She started pointing around the room declaring this came from such and such, and oh yeah, this came from...

Her room was full of trinkets all gifted from the different men she had been with...or, was currently with.

I was curious about the men she was currently with and wondered what they thought of her "collection."

With a little giggle she sheepishly said, "That is why I have to keep them in order."

My mind was spinning, desperately trying to put the pieces of this foreign puzzle together. The puzzle was not only unfamiliar to me but I did not have the blueprint. I had a very difficult time holding the pieces of her story together in my mind.

"So you have many boyfriends, guys, dates, customers...at the same time?" I didn't know the appropriate way to label them.

I finally settled on boyfriend because that was the term she used. Oy looked at me oddly and said "yes" as if I was the weird one.

I think my mouth hit the floor when she told me she was dating twelve men currently. No wonder she needed to keep them in order. It was for her sanity.

I do not know how she kept it all straight. I had enough trouble keeping dates straight with my *one* relationship.

I learned that each of her boyfriends was a paying customer. However, Oy saw them as more. She was choosing these relationships to further her goals. To her, there was strategy in milking the system for all it was worth. She worked the system to benefit her goals.

Oy would stay in touch with every single one of them. She did not want to lose the connection—or the money.

I was enthralled at her audaciousness. She talked about how she would meet up with one guy just for holidays throughout the year. He would pay for her to fly and for all accommodations and food. In return, she kept him company, translated, and was his tour guide.

Another guy she met with on weekends only.

She even stayed in touch with some of her boyfriends via Skype. They would wire her money and visit her one to two times a year. Oy did not have any negative qualms with the idea of having multiple boyfriends at the same time. She talked about it in such a way it seemed like a game to her. She was meticulous in keeping her life sorted.

Each man had a turn.

Each relationship felt monogamous.

Oy even shared how a foreign customer was better. They were less drama than the Thai men. She also said they treated her well and gave more money. I couldn't believe all the juggling was worth it to her. It seemed like so much work. Oy shared it in a way that made me think her life was good, beautiful even. This conflicted with other experiences of hopelessness and pain that I witnessed on a weekly basis.

She moved on to talk about her family. Her mom. Her brother. She loved them so much. She sent most of her money to them. They did not know what she did. They only knew she was doing well because of all she sent home. She had not seen them in years.

Proudly, she pulled out a photo album and showed me a picture that her mom had sent. The pictures in the album were of a home. The pictures held a chronological story of the construction of a house. The last picture was the home completed. Oy beamed as she talked. She had sent enough money home for her mom to get a house built.

She had paid for it all. Incredible!

She then went on to describe the money she sent to her brother and how he used it to buy a car. I had no words as I flipped through the album looking at the finished house and little blue hatchback.

I started to question Oy's intentions of hanging out with me. She knew I worked for an organization that helped girls and children escape the negative effects of prostitution, sex trafficking, and exploitation. Oy seemed to have a life she loved. For the first time, I was faced with someone who seemed to be doing very well financially. This experience was going against the status quo. What was I to think? Was there something hidden? Was I missing something?

As my brain tried rearranging my experiences to create something that logically made sense, my heart spoke. She reminded me that we are all searching for something. My friend was searching for something. This is why, time and time again, she joined many of our events. At each event, she wanted to know more about our mission and our team.

I left my thoughts at that.

Who am I? I did not know. I did not want to judge. Wasn't it enough to just enjoy the moment and be friends?

I was tired of analyzing. Tired of trying to figure things out. It was fascinating yet exhausting at the same time. I smiled to myself as I allowed this unresolved mystery to fade away so that I could enjoy the rest of my day with my friend Oy. That is exactly what I did.

Oy was the perfect hostess. We had some snacks, finished up my nails and then shared more about our families. I walked away from that date possibly more confused in some areas but definitely more confirmed in one area: I was overwhelmed with love.

The burning in my heart. The fire I felt—the passion deep inside. Something was going to come out of this. This feeling came when I went out at night and spent time with ladies like Oy. Love burst through. Love kept me coming back for more. Love kept me grounded in my actions.

Love said, "You matter."

Love took a risk. Love reached out. Love tried. Love was the sweet ring on my phone. Love was the time spent, the nails done, the snacks had and the laughs out loud. Love worked. Love sacrificed. Love was present.

I could feel it. I could taste it. I knew it. It amazed me that love found its way through people, places, and circumstances beyond my logic.

After my experience with Oy, I was bombarded by quite a few experiences that gave me a glimpse of ugly. How even the victims were overtaken by it.

It was survival and maybe just human nature and greed. The truth is brokenness creates brokenness. Pain brings on more pain. I struggled with seeing this in a victim.

I knew through my training and experience that no one ever got to that place of ugly except through some sort of trauma or painful life-altering experience. We have no problem labeling a perpetrator "ugly." We have no problem judging and pointing our fingers. There are very few of us who would judge in that same way in regard to talking or thinking about ugly and evil in the forms of people and persons considered victims.

In some sense, rightly so.

I have experienced ugly in every area of society. Hurting people bleed pain, wreak havoc, and pass on brokenness. It is a messy truth. I pondered Oy's story for days after our time together. Did she fit this? I knew I may never find out the answers.

I continued to meet with Oy. I learned that she'd been—and still is—married. Her husband works and lives in another area of Thailand. She visits him periodically. He does not know what she does.

Lies? Conceit? Unfaithfulness? Cheating? Did I see this as ugly when I connected them to my friend I cherished so much?

I constantly wrestled with my beliefs. I wrestled with what appeared in front of me and what I knew internally. What about the ladies I met within the brothels? Amongst themselves, they claimed to be friends. Were they true friends who had each other's back? Who did they burn trying to get a foot up? What about their lies?

Sharing some parts and withholding other parts of their work as they recruited gullible young girls from poor families and villages...seemed...well, I wasn't sure. These were women I had come to love. It was hard for me to associate them with dishonesty.

Though I saw so much beauty around, the evil came in shapes and sizes I was not used to. I found myself in a constant   struggle.   The   evil inside surfaced and bobbed back under, coming up for air time and time again. I had never been aware of it. I saw it in some of my conclusions; I found it trying to take sides. My judgments of others led me to see the ugly in myself. I saw evil and it was everywhere. No one was exempt, including myself.

Beauty was everywhere, too. I had to see the evil in others differently. I knew, I had experienced in that same place, in those same people, in myself, goodness and love. I turned the evil versus good and the black versus white into brokenness. I saw *our* brokenness.

We are all so wounded. It is not so divided. It is not easy to navigate. Brokenness is messy. There is not a right way but each has a roadmap. These maps take us down different paths—paths that we hope lead us to some sort of wholeness and healing.

Oy was looking for that, just as I was—something that could mend a huge gaping open heart wound, something that could heal. We wanted to bring back to life what the evil within had burnt down. We each have some area in our lives that we want to make right. Sometimes we see the evil pop up for air and we are appalled at what we see. But it's there.

The more I saw and experienced, the more I knew what it was that kept me coming back. Love. Love can heal. Love can mend. Love can put pieces back together. Love restores the shattered parts of our lives, the parts we don't let anyone know about. From that desire, we can reach out to others. It comes from a place where we hold on to hope.

Deep down we feel there is something out there that can heal—that will work. Some of us, without knowing it, have experienced it firsthand. Love restores and brings life.

chapter ten

A WOMAN'S WORTH

I knew I was barely scratching the surface of the complexity involved. Every night I would come home, I would download onto my husband for hours. Sometimes it was gut-wrenching and felt like my heart could not handle the force of the blow. I felt hurt so deep, so piercing, so uninvited I could only sob uncontrollably. He was always there to wipe my tears and listen. Life seemed so unfair at times.

It was unpredictable, cruel, and yet in the midst there were beautiful moments.

Some nights I would come home on a high, sitting on cloud nine. I was energized and vocalizing a million words a minute like the Energizer bunny. My thoughts could not keep up with my words. At these times, I would focus on moments—beautiful snapshots that I would forever hold in my mind.

My process of debriefing always involved getting everything out. The questions, the lack of answers, the unresolved issues, the pain, the hurt, the mourning, the suffering, my observations, my feelings, my thoughts...I held nothing back. I shared my shortcomings and my own ugliness. The parallels I would see between myself and the girls. I would share about the injustice I witnessed and then my feelings of intense hate. I would often times find myself feeling hopeless as I shared.

In my process there were always moments of courage and leaps of faith. I would beat myself up over my lack of language and the bloopers I would make. I would reenergize myself when I shared of the moments that brought smiles and laughs. The games and the conversations, it would all spill out until there was nothing left inside.

I was the garbage truck that filled with each passing hour of the night. When I finished and found myself at home, I needed space to sort and recycle. Eventually everything needed to be dumped. This was where my husband came into the picture.

There was so much inside—lots of it ugly, lots of mess, lots of wounds and yet some things were so perfect and beautiful. The only way to find what can be reused or salvaged is to dig. Debriefing was just that for me. It was my dumpster dive. I used it as a time to work through the evil and find the beauty. It was a great treasure hunt. My goal was to find a gem that had been hidden and lost.

Every night I went out, I dug and I dug. The going was rough. The heat was intense. The smells curled my nose and gripped my breath. I found myself moving, looking, searching for that hidden treasure. I would find it every single time I went out.

I found value.

I found women and men, boys and girls who *mattered*. They were worth the dig. They were worth the search. They were worth sorting through the evil piles of mess and brokenness, wounds and pain.

That is what I always circled back around to. People mattered. Wherever there is value, there is love. Love was the light that led me. Love was the beauty I knew I would find. Love would be the light in the darkness and the good in the midst of evil. Where you see love, you will find hope. Where there is love, there is restoration. Where there is love, there is healing and mending for the broken. Each experience I had solidified this fact to me. Evil highlighted my vain attempts and lack of understanding. Love compelled me to let go of my judgments.

One night in particular, I was tested yet again. It had been months of visiting this particular bar and unlike others it was different. I had become all too familiar with the normal bar scene. Each experience seemed to mirror the bar next to it. The music, the girls' dress, the types of customers that would come in and exit. The common nightly occurrences of drunk men and bar fights. I would be surrounded by girls with hollow eyes and minimal expressions. I could tell those who were seasoned and experienced and those who were new. The difference in this bar peaked my curiosity the very first time I stepped foot into it.

The difference had me coming back time and time again. Often, my teammates would want to go to other bars because "nothing" really happened here. It was this exact contrast to other bars that drew me in. I couldn't believe it at face value. I felt there was something under the surface. I found this bar to be the most tedious location and toughest challenge I had experienced.

For better terms this bar lacked excitement. It was hard to find information. The bar was the biggest on the strip. It was also the most packed every night. The girls were busy all the time. The other difference I immediately observed was the bar's extreme professionalism.

All the girls spoke English very well. They dressed in conservative uniforms. Their uniforms were similar to Thai university uniforms, with a small twist. Black skirts and instead of the pressed white button down collared shirt for school, these girls had on matching loose short sleeve polo shirts. There was hardly any skin. It was a bit odd in the middle of sexual tourism at its height.

It was hard to chat with any of the girls working there. They were consistently busy serving customers. Many nights I would sit at a table eating fries and drinking water, just observing in silence. I never saw any of the girls go off with any of the men. I had so many questions and thoughts. My curiosity kept me coming back for more. My digging finally paid off.

One night I arrived a bit early before the crowd and got to talk with two of the girls.

By this time, I do not think I was ever truly shocked by much of anything I saw, heard, or learned. I was, however, moved. My feelings ran deep. My feelings consumed and took over.

I remember sitting and listening as those two girls talked. *How is this possible?* They were both married. I had heard of this before, and through Oy, but I still found it confusing. The patterns and similarities were common amongst many of the girls I met. These two had husbands in their hometowns. One of them had a son that was living with her husband's parents and going to school. She would see him monthly. The other girl had a three-year-old son who lived with her. She was raising him as a single mom.

My conversations began to conflict with other beliefs I unknowingly held based on previous experiences growing up.

Based on my experience, single moms have it hard. I saw it every day growing up in the inner city amongst poverty, abuse, and lack of father figures. These moms are some of the strongest, most beautiful souls I have ever met. I would definitely want them on my side in any type of battle. Their strength and love and determination is admirable. As I pondered my encounters, thoughts of poverty and lack of education came to the forefront of my mind.

I found it hard to concentrate as I listened to my two new friends. Many of the things they were sharing did not fit inside my box—a box I had unknowing created. I began getting distracted. I was trying to find supporting evidence through my friends' conversations. What I was not doing was listening.

They would say things that bumped me. I thought I knew what girls who worked in the prostitution and sex tourism looked like. I thought I knew much of their history. I felt pretty convinced I knew their struggle.

I was so very wrong.

I had such strong images and beliefs. I tried sorting through them. As my awareness of these judgments grew, I began to feel queasy inside. It felt like the smell of trash. They wanted the spotlight. Inside, a battle raged. I wanted their stories—I always wanted their stories. My judgments wanted the win.

I halted my thoughts.

I vowed to listen.

There is always more than what meets the eye, I reminded myself. Soon I was again lost in our conversation.

Both of my new friends had university degrees. This was a first for me. One had a degree in science and the other in management. One worked in the hotel industry, which is one of the top paying jobs in Thailand. The other worked at a private international school as a teacher. *Wow.* I found my mind grappling with the information and the location where we were talking. Here we were sitting in an open-air, outdoor bar, nestled in a dark alley with no street lights. Not only that, global statistics show Southeast Asia as the heart of our world's global epidemic of modern-day slavery. Knowing this information kept me intrigued.

There is always more than what meets the eye.

The bar started to get full and I began getting many curious glances my way. I even noticed some of the men customers eavesdropping on our conversation. It did not bother me. I was lost in their story. Lost in the value of them. I wanted with all my heart that they would see value. I wanted to know them and for them to be known. It is what flowed from the depths of my heart, where no one saw it but where only I felt it. It felt just as real as the beating of my heart and the air my breath would suck in, moment by moment.

Soon I was only talking to one girl, Kim, as the other had to get up and work.

I flooded her with questions. "What brought you here? How long have you been working here? How do you compare this and your other job? Do you like this job?"

I have been on the receiving end of assumptions... the ones I remember are deep and painful. They usually involve an assumption or stereotype or belief that someone had of me. Instead of asking me a question they would talk to me using words in our conversations that brought out their assumptions. I have felt victimized and bombarded with these untruths. Many times it is from friends and loved ones—I don't know what's worse: being questioned by family or a stranger.

At the time, I desperately wished they would just ask me their questions. I try to do that with others. I am far from mastering this skill, especially while sitting in an unfamiliar place, surrounded by a different culture, religion, and way of life. This realization created a force that caused me to be aware, to slow down, and to think before I talked. This is a big reason why I watch —observe.

These tools are some of my greatest weapons in the war against human trafficking and exploitation.

These are some of the unseen and unspoken gifts I received during my time with my new friend Kim. I continued to frequent that bar and meet with her. She was smart, intelligent, well spoken, polished and professional. She was an amazing mom and great hostess. She was not struggling, actually quite the opposite, she was successful.

She had a high social status amongst her peers and family in the small village she grew up in. She was educated. She had a high paying, highly coveted job at an international school. Life looked good from that viewpoint. But the finances and demands of life with her son and taking care of her parents became too demanding. The never-ending stress of money caused her to look elsewhere for work which landed her at this bar sitting across from me.

She had been working here for eight months and was making more money than her "successful job" as an international school teacher. She spoke English, had a university degree, and taught at one of the highest paying schools in Thailand.

It was no easy feat to take her story in. I would look up to see the blackened windows of the brothel across the street looming tall and haunted...unwanted images raced across my mind. Behind those walls were trapped women, a stage that humans—numbers—paraded on. I had been there. I had witnessed and experienced the truth behind those walls. I felt the deep panic of memories rise inside of me.

The deafening roar and the powerful force hit me. It was like a tidal wave rushing over me. Many of these girls would sink to a low place after time had passed. They would believe that number pinned to them represented their worth, that they were just that: a number. Nothing more and nothing less. The very thought brought me nightmares.

Yet here I was, sitting in front of a woman who

knew her worth and wanted more. She had found her "more" in a place that—in my experience—stole one's value. She seemed happy on the outside and very happy for the funds she was earning. That was the part I had not figured out yet. How was she getting money?

Answers came slowly, and digging was long and tedious. Trust needed to be built. Time needed to be invested and stable consistencies were an absolute necessity. So many walls, so many experiences, and so many new faces coming and going for these ladies and children. I always found I never got the full story. I would always have to piece the stories together. Most of the conversations did not get to the depths, or expose the painful wounds.

I had a baby, and did not continue to visit Kim. I never had an opportunity to hear her entire story. Sometimes I still wrestle with it. Was she exploited? Was she at risk? Was she vulnerable? I have to answer "yes" to all the above.

I saw a country that neither pays a woman for her worth, nor rewards her for her education. A world that saw her as a weak link. She was vulnerable. She was discriminated against. She was marginalized. She was known for what she gave and not for who she was. Her immeasurable worth was swept away.

The place in which she found value, the bar scene in the heart of sex tourism, exploitation, and trafficking, could lead to unimaginable risk. She could find herself mixed up in unexpected situations and messiness.

I can only hope and pray she is safe—that her son is provided for and she is valued by someone. I pray that she is treated with honor and dignity.

Modern-day slavery exemplifies the ugliness in our world. It sheds light and brings to the forefront the injustice in society—injustice that preys on the weak. It feeds off poverty and lack of opportunities. It gains momentum by controlling the vulnerable. Those with privilege, wealth, and power supply it.

We know who they are...the ones that find themselves in its tightly clenched fist. They never asked for it, never wanted it, but are *born* into it. It affects our own world. Our workforce, our schools, our opportunities, and maybe our friends. They are women, they are children, they are minorities. They exist in every society.

The plight of these is daunting and exhausting if not almost an impossible feat. The immeasurable obstacles one has to face to move out and on to something better. The stereotypes, the worldview. I know this intimately. As a minority woman, I married internationally and have children born in a third culture. Our family speaks three languages and counting. It is sometimes hard to put into words the feeling of being less than enough—of feeling devalued and small. This is hard to sort through and navigate.

This is the place we stay away from. It hurts too much. I know this all too well. There is a feeling of no return. It's a current that sweeps you under. That feeling of despair. Like a candle, the small light of hope that casts its glow, lighting your path can just as quickly, in one moment, be blown out and the darkness surrounds you like a panic that takes over. The will to go on is just a small smoke signal billowing upwards in the unknown abyss of darkness. The feeling of being so worthless. The feeling that your value is so small. The feeling of being nothing in a room full of others who don't take you seriously. I find many times it is just a feeling. It is subtle. It is rarely direct, but the blow is brutal. The invisible nature of it speaks loudly. It speaks of systems, corruption and discrimination that are so embedded, the root of the issue is never addressed.

I have found over and over, similar stories from women and from minorities of those feelings of being devalued. They are confirmed when the pay is not the same. It is a stab in the heart to hear over and over of organizations and companies who speak on support and champion diversity and equality and yet those in positions of leadership and power lack the very things being championed. The hole is dug even deeper still when it branches off to equality for those who speak a different language, have different customs, and different religions. We talk a big talk and still have not found the courage to walk it out. The courage to face our own ugliness. The bravery to see with new eyes our own prejudices. Until we can turn the magnifying glass onto ourselves, we will never see the value in difference. We will not know how to appreciate with our actions and our words the beauty found in doing things and tackling problems from a different worldview. Our lack of knowledge and understanding about others has been a crutch–a sad, sad excuse. It is time to push through our fears and replace it with mystery and wonder and an attitude of learning.

Let's put ourselves in uncomfortable situations, let's place ourselves around people that have extreme differences. Only then will we see our own ugliness and only then can we, as a society, truly find value.

With patience and love, the treasure can be found, and drawn out for all of us to see. It will require going deep into the darkness of brokenness where pain lives. The wound has tormented and festered for a while. With humility and great courage, love is the only weapon we have that can restore. Love looks like worth and value. Love elevates and appreciates. It finds the beauty in the difference and praises it. Love embraces the difference, the mess, the fear. Love is the power that we have yet to unleash on a broken, dying world.

chapter eleven

BROKEN FAMILY

I live in a small village outside the city. It is a traditional village with modern touches. The village has paved roads and recently had a fundraiser to get street lights put up. Our neighborhood with modern homes was fortified with a guard and gate at the entrance of the village. Outside our neighborhood, the main street has a mix of traditional Thai houses and modern ones sprinkled in between. In the middle of every village in Thailand is a temple. With temples comes the common visual of monks clothed in orange robes.

Many monks will stay at the temple and keep it clean. Everyone is informed of the village news via announcements and prayers being chanted over loudspeakers. The loudspeakers were positioned throughout the village including in our neighborhood. Each day I listened to the tropical birds sing their chorus, smelled the flowers through the open windows and at 6:00 a.m. sharp, over loudspeakers, I would listen to the Thai national anthem.

There is a school next to the temple. Most of the children arrive by walking or by sitting on the seat of a bicycle while their grandmothers ride with them to school. Homes in the village tend to be multi-generational families living together under one roof. The younger generation worked in the city and the grandparents stayed home with the little ones while taking care of the home and garden.

My neighborhood is safe and quiet. On any given day, I usually notice everyone spends some time gardening and watering their plants. There is a time of sweeping fallen leafs and flowers off the driveways outside. Each weekend most neighbors have all their laundry hanging outside to dry. Many get their exercise after the sun goes down at 6:00 p.m. by walking or bicycling through the village. There are only two homes on our entire street that are not owned, but rented; ours is one of them. I have lived here for seven years and counting. I love my neighbors. They are everything one would want in kindness, thoughtfulness, and helpfulness.

Pi Naa across the street, an elderly lady who underwent a mastectomy, comes over to our yard on a weekly basis and sweeps all the leaves off our driveway. Lung, her daughter-in-law, is very extroverted and took no time to make me feel at home when we first moved here. Lung's English was very good at the time.

I started seeing Lung on a daily basis and in a week or so we were eating meals together almost every other day. If we were not eating together, we were bringing food over to each other. This is a Thai tradition that was passed from her to me. I am often seen walking through our neighborhood giving out fresh treats or "new" foods to try from America.

After months of hanging out with Lung and piecing her story together, I came home flabbergasted. I couldn't wait to talk to my husband. What I learned sent my head spinning.

Lung liked going out every weekend. Her favorite places to go were dance clubs and bars. She invited me out with her multiple times but I kindly refused. I found it more enjoyable to chat and eat together. I am not a dancer. I hate loud music and never really went clubbing...unless it was the quickie bar.

One evening over a meal I asked Lung what area of town the clubs and bars were located. Lung proceeded to tell me three to four different bars she liked going to and their location. To my surprise, I knew those bars. Those bars were located in the heart of our city's red light districts. My mind raced. Why was she hanging out *there*?

I had friends that worked at those bars. I frequented those bars nightly for work! Those bars had become my second home! Here I was sitting in a normal Thai home —a home situated outside the city in a small village— eating a normal meal with my normal neighbor. Only now it did not seem *normal*.

My neighbor, my friend, my same-aged peer, happily married and financially secure, was frequenting bars and clubs in the main red light district. Weekly. Only one thing happens there.

It is never what it seems.

I found my thoughts bouncing from one experience to another. I could not land on anything definitive. There were so many curve balls surrounding my world in Thailand. What I found was so crazy how I continued to see glimpses of this brokenness everywhere. Its reaches were far and wide.

In some way every single person I have met has been affected by its grasp.

My friend continued to tell me proudly how she learned English there by meeting foreign guys. I couldn't believe it. In my gut, I knew that "meeting" meant something entirely different. Yet this was how she told her story.

Lung held back no details. To her, this was her life. She seemed to talk in a way that made it a common fact. If anyone else were to be sitting on her bed listening to what I was, words would surely have escaped them. I know if I had had this conversation with her months earlier it would have sent me on a mental rollercoaster ride. I would have found myself trying to navigate and decide where the friendship would go. I would have asked myself if she would be a good friend to continue hanging out with.

All the times I rubbed shoulders with person after person softened me. I found myself less judgmental and more open to understanding. My mind did not question everything to the extent it used to. I found myself full of compassion, empathy and I had a feeling that I just didn't know the full story. I wanted to know that story— but does that surprise you at this point?

At that moment I was thankful for my experiences. I was able to roll with her story very easily. I was not as surprised as I would have been hearing it for the first time. Part of me felt a bit surreal that I was across the street from my small home nestled inside an ordinary neighborhood interacting with my friend, who was meeting guys at bars located in the red light districts.

Lung was dating a foreigner that she met at one of those bars. Lung was also married to another man. Lung lived with her husband. She had been married for six years. At the time, that was how long my husband and I had been married. She would say "happily married."

Lung told me this in front of her family and husband. She spoke kindly about her husband and rubbed his hand while she talked.

Lung then spoke about her boyfriend *in front* of her husband.

I didn't know how to join the conversation. It was so foreign to me. I felt like an outsider. It didn't seem right to me. When her husband got up to bring more food or drinks, I used the time to ask questions.

I asked what her husband thought about her dating someone. Nonchalantly, she said it was okay because she knew he was seeing someone where he worked. They were both happy, she finished. It was mind-blowing to me. I could not fathom my relationship working in this way.

In a later conversation I found out Lung wanted more out of relationships and life. She wanted passion. She wanted adventure. Her husband wanted children and she did not. It seemed a mutual agreement between the two of them that *this* was acceptable. It shed light on the family structure in Thailand.

My time in Thailand has shown me the status of a

crumbling family unit. It far exceeds our western world's definition of family problems. It is extremely hard to see unless one is looking for it. It is hidden in plain sight. Marriage is not a sacred covenant. Marriage is not always about love. Many times, it is but a necessity to carry the family name on. It ensures one's retirement plan. The younger generation takes care of the older generation. Marriage and children ensure you will be taken care of. There is not a cultural home care for the elderly.

My experience and observation of family in America is starkly different than what I witness in Thailand. In Thailand there is marriage by paper. There are also marriages without any documentation. Multiple wives are acceptable if the husband can provide for each. I do not hear the word "divorce" when I roam the corners.

If a man leaves his wife, there is no accountability for him to provide for or financially help any of his children. Many times the wife will find another man who can help provide financially. There are splits and separations, but very rarely do I hear people actually use the word "divorce." The downside of this involves the children. Many new "husbands" will not take on children from previous relationships. Lots of these children end up in orphanages and children's homes. It is sad—particularly when the majority of these children have parents.

Now there are husbands with multiple wives.

Eventually, a man might find his wife requires too much from him and he feels the fun has left. So, he will then find a girlfriend...while still married. Most women subjected to this lifestyle see this as normal.

It is so normal, in fact, that when my husband and I are out together we get asked about it. It usually comes up during a conversation with friends. While talking, our friends will want to know when my husband will see his other wife or girlfriend. It blows me away every time. Some of our friends who ask this know how long we have been married! My husband always shakes his head and answers that he only has *one* wife: me. No girlfriends. That answer leaves our friends speechless.

I learned that the "girlfriends" do not get as much money. A man will see her certain days of the week, take her out, and pursue her. Many Thai men feel sexually unsatisfied with these two types of relationships. They also have the opportunity to find a "gig." This is commonly known to us from the west as a friend with benefits.

There will be an arrangement for certain times with no strings attached. This relationship will cost even less than a girlfriend. The time spent will also be less. The relationship will not go very deep. Now, we have a man with multiple wives, a girlfriend, and a friend with benefits. To finish the "family unit" lastly comes the prostitute. He will visit with them whenever he wants.

Many think the huge issues of sexual exploitation in many forms come from outside Thailand. This could not be farther from the truth in my opinion. The many issues surrounding modern-day slavery come from within. Sexual tourism is a billion-dollar industry in Thailand. I believe it stays alive because it is fed from within. It is a deep internal issue. Thai men keep the system and the exploitation spinning. More Thai men frequent prostitutes each year than foreign men. However, foreign men pay more for theirs. Asia, in general, has deep ties to the sexualization and exploitation of women and children from Japan to Malaysia.

This is a more in-depth view of family in Thailand. My friend Lung's story was quite normal to her and to anyone she may have shared it with there.

Marriage in Thailand is complicated and has many layers and components to it. One thing, however, is staggering. In a country where sexuality can blatantly hit you smack in the face it hides a deep, dark secret. Thai marriages have the least amount of sex in the whole world. Shocking. That is how I felt when I heard that the first time. However, the more I learned and the deeper I got, it makes perfect sense. A Thai person's first introduction of sexuality is never in the "commitment" or confines of marriage. They are left to navigate it from another playing field.

My husband and I were part of creating a survey. It was passed out to students at multiple universities in our city. In this survey, we asked some very personal and probing questions about their sexual preferences, their families, pornography, birth control, masturbation, and sex encounters. The findings and feedback were extremely insightful for me.

One number stood out to me the most. Nine out of ten university age students were exploring their sexuality. They did not have a gender preference with whom they slept with. It could be male or female. We did a follow-up questionnaire on this one result. On the follow-up, we found that it was acceptable to "figure out" and explore during this age and stage in life. However, once one reaches thirty, they need to "settle down" and get married to start a family. This is the path many Thai go down. There are those who choose another path, too.

Some choose to go the lady boy route. This is a completely acceptable option for a Thai. I have seen in my years in Thailand how the gender roles are so defined and strong. The option of being a lady boy is a breath of fresh air for many. It allows them to navigate their own self and not conform to such strong gender norms. In a society that is extremely kind and warm, it lacks emotional depth in relationships. A lady boy can express and be emotional. He can be the Thai who has passion and who feels. With this third gender in Thailand there is a place for people to express themselves. They do not have to conform to the social boxes and stereotypes the rest of the population subconsciously abides by.

One of the most fascinating topics I see played out in such a different way in Thailand vs. the western world is the life and experience of the LGBT community. In American, this community is not recognized in many areas and they are fighting for their rights. I would suggest that religion and beliefs play a part. It can be seen all the way down to the "creation story" and its intricate role in the shaping of American society. In Thailand, the creation story involves three genders—the third gender being a lady boy. From the beginning it has found a place and is acceptable.

In Thailand, those that choose this path are not fighting for their rights. They, in a sense, are discovering themselves and have full freedom to do so in that manner for however long or short they want to. Some live the lifestyle for only a matter of years. Others continue with hormone injection and full sex change surgery, Thailand being one of the leading countries in performing this type of surgery.

In Thailand, the gay parades and rainbow flags staked at homes and businesses do not exist. The local people do not need it. They do not have an agenda to advance. They can use whichever bathrooms they want and can change their name and license whenever they want. For a Thai, they can have any job they want, live where they want, be with whomever they want, and it is not looked down upon and not discriminated against. Many times they will be the first to get hired and the life of the party. So why does it really matter? I believe it's necessary to see all the forms of sexuality in a country and culture and see how it plays a part in the evil sides of sexual exploitation.

Thailand is one of the top countries with a huge divide in economic class issues. Issues that perpetuate poverty and the ugly cycle of modern-day slavery. I think understanding the sexual culture is necessary to help find solutions. And maybe, just maybe, the family unit plays a big part in that solution.

Thailand is known as the land of smiles, yet culturally, their biggest priority is to keep a good face. This means the outside needs to look right. If something is looking bad, there needs to be an immediate fix. Usually the fix does not address the root of the problem, it is merely a nice Band-Aid to keep the ugly wound from the public eye. I believe this happens concerning sexuality and all the ugly associated with it in Thailand. In the western world, we have become more horrified of the crimes done to children by leaders in religious positions.

It seems every week one just needs to open the paper or listen to the radio or watch the news and abuse and exploitation is rampant in safe places like the church. These spiritual havens have many hidden secrets. It is the same in Thailand. In some sense, it is worse because the light does not get shed on it as much. It is also a common occurrence in monasteries with monks. There will be an occasional story in the Thai newspaper. The story will only appear if it is really big news that cannot be covered. Many do not get detected. I am heartbroken every year I live in Thailand and the truth of this reality is ever present.

Between molestation, sexual abuse, rape, incest, exploitation sexually, labor, kidnapping, trafficking, poor education (Thailand is the second lowest in the world), and poverty, children have a huge mountain to climb in Thailand. In my time in Thailand, those I have personally invested in and rubbed shoulders with, eight out of ten were sexually abused as children. Most by family members. For many of them, it happened at school.

Security at schools is very low and almost nonexistent by our western standards. My husband used to work at a Thai school teaching first graders and more than once he witnessed screams coming from the bathroom. The school security would then be seen dragging a man out covered in a sheet—he had been hiding in the bathroom, naked, waiting for his next victim.

I have firsthand experience from sending my children to an all Thai school. They were the only foreigners attending. One day, after school, my son shared about how he had been touched inappropriately by his teacher. I found myself confronted with the fact that there are no policies in place for this situation at most of the Thai schools. There are also no safety codes for school buildings. Things like guest passes or locked doors are not guaranteed. Many schools are open air and usually have a fence with an open gate around the yard. Children are extremely vulnerable and at high risk of abuse and exploitation in their normal lives.

This insight I have gleaned over my time living in Thailand has continually impressed on my heart two things. The first, there is much to be done in Thailand. I believe changes within normal, everyday life and learning can play a huge impact on modern-day slavery. Second, the fabric of Thai society has so many holes in how families operate and how vulnerable children are, it's no wonder Thailand is a breeding ground for so much exploitation.

chapter twelve

A Mother's Love

The love of a mother is such a strong image and picture. Her love is fierce and defies logic. A mother's love not only has a power that will not fail. Her love shows us what is valuable. I am forever indebted to the countless ladies I met during my years working in some of the darkest places in our world. Women who lived this, who modeled this. The great power they embodied loving their children in the midst of surviving. What they sacrificed spoke volumes to me. I know it has shaped me as a mother. Their fierce determination and unwavering commitment to their children was so heroic to me, I would be overtaken with emotion time and time again. Nothing showed this to me stronger than when I met my friend Ana. When nothing around me seemed lovely, Ana's expression of love left me in tears.

Ana was not her real name, just like every other name I have written in here. The Thai go by many names in their lifetime. They usually changing them when they change jobs, move or even have new friends. Most birth names in Thai are so long it is hard to remember them. Many have adopted short easy names.

I remember distinctly when I met Ana at "Blu Bar" just a couple establishments away from where I would hang out with the street kids on the corners some nights. Ana was hospitable, cordial, and polite. Her English was amazing. She was not loud and obnoxious like some of the other ladies, demanding attention. She had confidence. I found out quickly that hope lived inside her. Hope that others could have it better. I am not sure where her hope came from. I imagine it was her life before I knew her. I never uncovered that piece of her history.

Ana saw life beyond the brothel. She had some freedom from working her way up the bar system ladder. Ana was one of the few ladies I met that would call me weekly. She would call to chat or to invite me somewhere. My first experience outside the brothel with Ana impacted me profoundly.

Ana picked me up one afternoon in a tuk tuk. She was taking me on an adventure. She would not tell me where. I honestly had no idea where we were going. She mentioned she would go to this spot whenever she had free time. We arrived at a small hole in the wall establishment sardined between two big townhouse styled shops. The little spot, with its exposed concrete walls and peeling blue paint, was literally a couple blocks from the brothel where Ana worked. To my amazement, inside was an orphanage. Home to ten little babies, all under the age of one.

They were the cutest, chubbiest bundles of sweetness. Ana introduced me to the Thai staff there and then we spent an hour playing on the floor. The babies slowly grew used to us and started climbing over our legs. As I sat there, I soaked up my surroundings. The inside was simple. There was one room, with metal bars on the one small window next to the door. There were whitewashed walls and tile floor. Against the wall was a line of small metal cribs. There were no bright colors or inviting decor. I did not see any blankets on the beds. There were no toys. It felt more like a hospital than a home. It was cold and dark.

The babies all had cloth diapers on. Some of the adventurous ones were soon trying to stand as we sat on the floor stabilizing them. Ana began to share with me that she volunteered here every month. She loved those babies. She would even give a percent of her money to them.

One little boy seemed quite attached to me. He found his way into my lap and fell asleep. Ana pointed to him and shared that he was going to be adopted next month. Ana was taking a plane ride with him to Bangkok to give him away. I cannot tell you how surprised I was in that moment.

Everything I "thought" I knew about my work and the many ladies, lady boys, and children I had encountered, none had ever been like Ana. Again, I was confronted with the many boxes and stereotypes I would subconsciously put around people. Yet here again I was humbled and honored to be in the presence of someone who had been through things I probably could never imagine and yet her love was fierce. It showed me a bright light in the darkness. I could have stayed for hours. The place was peaceful. There were not any crying babies. There was an empty feeling though. I also had a lump in my stomach when I left, having never seen one baby smile. I was not able to process my time right away because Ana had another adventure she was taking me on.

We took off again, weaving in and out of cars, motorbikes, bicycles and big trucks. We drove past the city limits into the country. I gazed at the open road. Rice fields on each side sped by and an occasional Thai house on stilts dotted the landscape. Water buffalo slowly chewing long grass would be knee deep in muddy ditch water trying to stay cool. I had no idea where we were going and did not expect to be on the road for two hours. The tuk tuk's smog was thick, black and smelly and its engine was too loud to hear each other's voices so I sat back and took in the scenery.

The Thai landscape has its own kind of beauty. How had I—a small-town girl from Nebraska—gotten here?

I was just as in awe of my own situation as I was of the mountains that I had fallen in love with. I had so much. I felt it was truly a privilege to be in that exact moment. I was overwhelmed with gratitude for the opportunity in front of me. I felt thankful for Ana. She made me want to sit back and take note of the small, wondrous miracles in life, the beauty in our world and in our surroundings. She gave me a dose of courage. A feeling that none of us is ever so bad off that we cannot think of another. That life is never so black it steals away our own choice to help or act in kindness in some way. Maybe this is what drew us to each other. Maybe this was the foundation of our relationship. Maybe this was why she was so different than the other girls for me. Our bond grew deeper that day, over one commonality, people matter. Their lives are worth fighting for. I saw it again as we pulled up to a huge building in the middle of nowhere...

This building was some sort of compound. The building was connected on all four sides. Inside was a huge grassy yard with a wooden playground in the middle. Children were everywhere. We were at another orphanage.

This was a unique place because these children had parents, yet they were orphans. Their mothers had remarried and the new husband wanted nothing to do with them. I had heard about this orphanage because it was started and run by western foreigners. It was a home for children that could not get adopted. This home provided education and opportunities to the children.

My friend knew one of the Thai staff working there. She had brought me all the way there because she thought I may want the connection. Since it was run by foreigners and many spoke English she thought some of my connections and English-speaking friends may want to help there too. Incredible. On her day off, when most girls were sleeping in, Ana was out volunteering and donating. I felt so much appreciation. Her thoughtfulness and selflessness were contagious.

As night fell, we finally made our way back to the city. We arrived back at Blu Bar where she worked. Once we landed, I finally had a chance to ask her the millions of questions that had been floating in my head all day. Where did this fierce love come from? Why did these children matter so much? Why did she do what she did? Soon, I found out. Sitting under the bright lights of the bar sign, I learned more about Ana's story.

Ana was a mother. She had a little boy who was not yet one year old. As she talked about her son her eyes began to fill with water and spill down her face. This was the first time in a month of hanging out with her I had seen any sort of emotion. These feelings took over her. I could feel the fierceness of her love as she talked about her son. I was not sure where and why the emotions were welling up. I wondered where her son was. Was he okay? I tried connecting the dots as Ana shared. Again, language barriers confused me. Again, past and present tenses were switched. I was not sure the exact scenario of what I was hearing. I waited until the right moment to clarify. I was trying to be sensitive in my question. Where is your son? To that, she responded that he was in Bangkok at an international school. School? I could not comprehend it.

I soon realized it was a "glorified daycare" with a twist. It was a daycare boarding school of some kind. I was very familiar with the idea of boarding school from living overseas. Many families that live in another country send their children off to boarding schools for a better education. I, however, had never heard of anyone sending such a young child away. It seemed odd to me. I fully believe a child that age needs a mother more than a school.

"What's the reason you send him there?" I asked Ana. "How does this benefit him and you?"

I was curious, baffled and could not accept the fact that an infant was thousands of miles away from his mother. A mother who obviously loved him so much. Ana replied with such a strong statement I felt at a loss of what to say next.

She bluntly told me that she could not be a good mother. She was "too young," and "did not know what to do." She went on to say that her son is getting the best education.

She was paying for his international school in hopes that he would grow up and have the best opportunities for jobs. I just couldn't take it. Her son needed her! I began to spill my thoughts. They rolled out without my permission. I didn't know how to check myself. I didn't censor my words. What I was seeing and hearing seemed so opposing. I am not sure she wanted to hear what I said. I just couldn't hold it back. I needed to speak.

I picked up both her hands. Locking my eyes with hers, tears started streaming down my cheeks. "You are a great mom! You love your son so much. You take care of all those babies and you do wonderfully. Your son needs you. Every mother is a first-time mother. No one knows what to do all the time. You are not too young. You can do this. All it takes is love.

No amount of conviction I felt could change her. I mustered everything I could think of. I pleaded. I tried to convince. I thought I was persuasive. I believe she must have spent countless hours thinking through this decision. She was very convinced that this was the best thing for him. She was sticking to it. Along the way, when times were hard, when every bone in her body ached for him, and the memories of his smell flooded her senses, she would find reasons why she was not enough for him. Ana filled her days doing what she thought was best to make it possible for him to have a better life than her.

The depths of my being could not comprehend her reason and her logic. There seemed to be none. Love always looks the same. The situation, people, and circumstances are different. Love fights, love gives everything. Love is stronger than pain and suffering. Love puts others ahead of ourselves. Love makes a way. A mother's love is one of the best and most in-depth models of love I believe we carry on this earth. I am so thankful for my friendship with Ana and the many ways her life modeled and taught me what love looks like.

chapter thirteen

Fortune Teller

I happened, one night, onto a table with a couple girls I had recently met and was getting to know. They were talking with someone. I slid onto the bench and joined the conversation. In front of me was a fortune teller. A modern-day witch and tarot card reader. I had known the Thai are very superstitious. It is obvious from their conversations and their many "wee ti's" (daily practices). The Thai do many spiritual acts throughout the day.

They will mark their cars on the inside dashboards and roof with painted dots in the shape of a triangle. This represents the way to Nirvana. They will buy flowers, while stopped at a red light, from poor individuals and children selling them. They will hang these flowers on their mirrors. Thai believe these practices will help protect them from car accidents.

Throughout the city one will notice many

handicapped and amputees sitting in their wheelchairs on the side of the road. In front of them or sitting on their lap will be a huge board or table. On this table will by rows of cards. These cards are a type of lottery card. The Thai love to purchase them on certain days.

If you drive through cities within Thailand you will usually come upon a tree with orange cloth wrapped around it. This signifies a spirit lives there. These trees are sacred. Some will even leave food, drinks, and candles at the foot of the tree. Each of these actions is very spiritual for a Thai.

I even found a fascinating correlation with my own birth story. I had my son naturally on February 22, 2012, the night of a full moon. The hospital was so packed and busy when I arrived heavy in labor they could not find an available room for me. I was later told that the date was a "special day" in Thailand. Many Thai women will visit a monk while pregnant. That monk will give her a blessing and bless the baby. Many times, the monk will also suggest a time and day when to have the baby for the best fortune. The Thai mother would then schedule a C-section for that time. This ensured that her baby had the best chance of a happy, successful life. Certain days on the Thai calendar would be "good luck" days to have a child. A full moon and the date was a combination that had women all over the city scheduling their births. It was so busy that I birthed my child in a non-birthing room. I was not moved into the recovery room until two days after my birth. In the villages, natural births are still abundant and normal, as hospitals may not be close by. This is a great picture of city living and modern-day spirituality at its best.

The Thai are very into "signs." The stars and numbers and horoscopes are common general conversations. I've been asked many times what my astrology sign is and my horoscope. I have found it fascinating that once I've communicated this, my friends would then connect the happenings in my life and my goals to it, all in an attempt to encourage me that my desired outcome will happen. I have been surprised at how ingrained it is in the culture even crossing economic status.

I've sat in brothels having conversations about navigating horoscopes and numbers. Without realizing it, those conversations did not affect me.

Subconsciously I realized I had a judgment that said, "because their situation is bad, they are looking for anything and everything to find hope for something better." It wasn't until I had the same conversation in a completely different environment I realized my judgment.

I have a group of Thai friends that are high class. They are young thirty-something entrepreneurs. As women, mothers, and wives they are inspiring. These friends travel all over the world year after year. Most of them studied university overseas. Each of them started their own business. I learned very quickly that fortune tellers and signs were a huge part in their life as well. Every single time I have ever met with any of them our conversation eventually turned to this topic. My successful, wealthy friends are just as committed to knowing and following any signs they see or are given. This is part of their spirituality and they culturally believe that it will truly benefit their path as they journey toward success and happiness. My friends also believe it directly impacts the safety and protection of their family.

The night I sat across from the fortune teller, next to my friends at a dim, cold "lower cast" bar for "newbies" was a night I will never forget. It was an experience that I've never had. Very outside my box. I had never spoken to anyone with these types of "insights" and "powers." I was brought up believing this world was false. I valued what I thought of as truth and looked down on superstition, the term I used to describe the idea of horoscopes and tarot cards. I sat at that table, curious. I had an appetite for new things. I know it was because I had friends who found it valuable. Since it was valuable to them, I wanted to see it from their eyes. I tried to keep my judgments down as I sat and listened.

The two friends I was sitting with had confided in me that they did not want to keep working at the bar. They both shared how they felt trapped. It was extremely vulnerable for them to share this with me. They both didn't see a way out. With this backdrop and insight, I sat quietly watching as the night began to unfold.

A fanned-out stack of cards were lined up, face down, on the table. Slowly, my friend Jip pulled out three cards. Next, my other friend Tip slid three cards out of the pile. With their cards chosen they pulled their hands back down into the folds of their laps. The fortune teller flipped the first card over. The space around our table was thick. Disco music and blaring lights were all around us, but we didn't notice it. The intense concentration and focus submersed us. You could have heard a pin drop. I was holding my breath. Thinking. Wondering. Waiting. What would the "seer" say? I do not remember the exact picture on the card. What I do remember was that it was dark and scary. I just knew it couldn't be good. The explanation of the card was given. In the card was death. No one spoke. All eyes were on the teller. I was trying to grasp hope.

Why would anyone want this? We all sat frozen. No one moved. No one spoke.

My friend's second card was read. This card was strikingly different in feeling and color. The teller shared that she was going to have a baby boy. I grappled for solid ground. How does one *know* these types of things? I felt so many emotions. The stronger emotions that took over were infuriation and anger. Who was this stranger who held life and death in her palm? Literally, she brought with her those feelings and emotions with each person she encountered. I saw it firsthand with my friends. They melted in her presence. What type of power did she possess? Why did my friends give this power to her? As my mind swirled in thoughts and my body temperature rose from emotions, I wondered what my friends were thinking and feeling.

I didn't have to wait long. Jip immediately ask if she should have an abortion. I did not see that one coming. The card was bright and beautiful. My first thought on hearing about a baby was beautiful, happy thoughts. How deceiving my view is.

I am forever surprised at how subconsciously assuming I am. I am forever shaped by my own experiences and my own beliefs, that I put them on others. It is but a split thought racing across my mind. One so small and yet so deceiving. I desire change. I am in continual pursuit of growth in this area. A good thing for me may not be good for someone else. How often I find myself giving advice based on what has worked for me. I intentionally chose to put this thought in check. I then wondered what the reason was that my friend suggested an abortion.

Jip explained how she wanted a girl. The fortune teller had said she was going to have a boy. Jip also didn't want to get pregnant now. As her thoughts spilled out to the fortune teller, I could feel a burning, deep inside me. It felt like there was some sort of injustice.

A baby's life was hanging in the balance. My friend and this fortune teller were having a conversation about a life not yet conceived. A life merely brought into existence by a card. In my mind, an "idea" at best. Not something that one should change their life over. I could see the stress building in my friend. It didn't seem right. In my opinion, there were a lot of *if*'s and uncertainty surrounding this very bizarre scenario. If my friend did get pregnant, it could very well be a girl. The intensity of the conversation escalated as my friend really seemed quite panicked. I couldn't stay quiet.

I needed to know why my friend would trust a total stranger. The way in which the fortune teller talked hinted that if my friend did have a baby girl it would not bring her good fortune. There was this underlying assumption. If the cards and advice were not followed, it would be bad for my friend.

Looking back, I believe I broke every cultural law of respect in this situation. I spoke directly and boldly at a person of extreme influence and power in Thai society. I was completely naive. I am sure I came off very brash. I demanded this teller to share how she could possibly know this information. How could she possibly see something that was not? Her answers were vague. She never addressed my questions. She would change the subject and move to another topic. There was nothing I could do at that point. I turned my energy toward silencing my inner thoughts and let the intense energy leave my body.

My other friend got enough courage to ask about her reading. The death card. I could see the fear in her eyes as she spoke. I could see how much hope and trust she gave to the Teller. I knew as I watched, in some weird way, that fortune teller had my friend's life in her hands. My friend was like a puppet on strings. The Teller could pull a string and my friend would move that way. I wanted to cry. It felt like another prison to me. At that moment, I saw the desperate need to know the future. The need overtook the possibility of a dark outcome. I waited for the Teller to answer.

"The death would come to someone close to you," came the ice-cold words.

The words hit like a boulder. The thought knocked the breath out of me. I could not stay quiet. How could someone be so insensitive? Why would someone say things that would bring evil onto someone? My thoughts brought me to boiling again. I couldn't stay quiet.

As I boiled over, my insides spilling out, I boldly asked, "How can you know? How can you be so sure?"

How can you tell my friend here such heart-wrenching news and just leave it at that? You claim to have some sort of power in seeing, do you have power for anything else?

I bombarded her with questions and she began to fidget in her seat. Her eyes shifted left and right. I could tell she didn't really want to talk with me. However, I was stunned when she got up and almost ran out.

Relief and bewilderment flooded over me. My friends and I all sat in stunned silence for what seemed a few minutes. When I looked up at my friends I saw their confusion. I sensed fear and uncertainty. I didn't like that feeling. I didn't want my friends left with those feelings. How could I address it? Was there any way to bring hope back? I wanted to understand more. Jip shared she was afraid of getting pregnant now. I could

143

feel her fear. I wanted to convince her she didn't need to keep it. Why did they give a stranger power? A human, a mortal, an unknown person who was paid. *Why?* I wanted to know why Jip would make a decision about aborting a baby on this tarot card reading, so I asked. My friend had no answers.

"It is what you do." That was the best explanation I received.

As a Thai, one will pay for a fortune teller with the hope to get lucky. For my friend, it was worth the try in hopes of a good fortune.

There is always the unknown, the bad news. I found their desire to know outweighed it all. I went home and began to see parallels in my own life. In my own spirituality and in my own culture. I believe we are all spiritual beings looking for meaning and deep understanding about complex topics. We feel, far too often, our lives are out of our control. Having a promise or something to stand on helps us feel somewhat grounded. I was not so different from my friends. I myself have pursued words of insight, many of these words spoken over me by strangers. Some of the words given to me brought life to my weary bones. Some of them felt empty.

I have spent my entire life believing in things that I cannot see. Doing this requires faith. I have stood on the unknown, promises given and words spoken over me. My spirituality takes on a different outward form but the basic building blocks are the same. My friends and I had a common need. We yearned for something out of our human grasp. We wanted a promise and good word. We wanted someone to blow life into our weary bones. We wanted someone to speak success and happiness over us.

I was more connected to my friends than I ever imagined. Words bring life and death. Somehow, they have that power. In desperate and successful times, we still yearn for them. Signs. Signs that everything is or will be alright. These words, when good, give us hope. They allow us to stand on something that feels solid. Allow us to move toward and achieve the unimaginable. I think love dwells in words. It abides in the words that bring life. Even in pain, loss, upsetting circumstances, or bleak outcomes, love operates through words that express hope and a future.

chapter fourteen

OPPORTUNITY

The feeling of being proud comes from love.

I have been so overtaken by her that it feels as if I could explode, like a firework shooting out light, color, action...its beauty is electrifying. It is a wonderful feeling and I have found myself in her space multiple times while training, teaching, and working with women who are at risk of sexual exploitation and trafficking.

At the organization I work with, we were always trying to expand and evolve our programs for the ladies. We offered a culinary school and hospitality school. Eventually, they evolved. One turned into a small event planning business. The other turned into a small bed and breakfast type retreat center. I helped teach and train in everything from making homemade pizzas to cookies and brownies. I smile every time I think about the fun I had doing this.

Most training in our culinary academy involved some type of cooking and the skills involved. We would practice cutting, dicing, heating, and measuring. Once in a while, we would train the girls in customer service and etiquette. Real events and parties accelerated the training. We would host baby showers and small dinner parties at our facility. During the events, our girls would get to practice their newly learned skills. I found so much joy and pride watching them.

I remember the first event we planned. It was to be our girls' first time on the floor. The back kitchen was filled with nervous energy, shy smiles, and timid chatter. They were so afraid, so insecure, so nervous. I tried my best to reassure them. I knew the party personally and they would more than gracious customers. We were hosting a baby shower. Small hors-d'oeuvres and drinks.

For me these types of events were thrilling. I had designed many parties and events myself. I liked to think of myself as a party planner. All the decor and set up was right up my alley. I knew without a shadow of a doubt, those moments at our school were moments where the girls forgot the situations they were in. They were moments where they could imagine, create, and believe in a new life. A new world of opportunity opened up to them. I could see it in their posture—their eyes. The stress would melt away as they became more comfortable with our staff and each other.

Each class began with timid, uncertain, and shy trainees. Whispers would fill the air. I would go from station to station helping measure and chop. Soon I would hear a small giggle. When the food went into the oven, it seemed, the atmosphere would shift. As we would all sit in anticipation, our guards would come down. We would start interacting and getting to know each other. Soon we would be laughing, covered in flour. The fun we all had waiting to get our first taste once it popped out of the oven. These moments were precious. A time where I was able to interact with the ladies in a safer and quieter atmosphere.

As the girls lined up, ready to go onto the floor for their first time, my heart skipped a beat. That feeling of pride, oh how it rose up inside of me. I stood breathlessly watching through a crack in the door. One by one the ladies walked out in their pressed uniforms. I knew how nervous they were.

Each girl found her spot on the floor.

I smiled as I watched them begin serving.

Some were physically shaking. It was inspiring to see them overcome their fears. I sat back and watched in awe. One began filling the water. I smiled as she draped the towel over her arm. She had not forgotten the small details. The night continued smoothly. Many of the girls collapsed in exhilaration once they emerged through the back kitchen doors. The thrill, fear, and energy would literally make them crumble. I remember trying my best to encourage and champion them.

The girls did fabulously. The courage, the strength, the spirit they had. I could feel it deep in my soul. It was like watching your own children tackle something that was challenging and see them overcome it. There is nothing so exhilarating. Nothing so inspiring. Nothing more beautiful than these girls that showed up. Alu-loa! (Samoan word that means to go and not hold back). This is how I saw them. A beautiful example of their unbreakable determination and grit.

If we did not have an event we were hosting, many times the treats we would make would be used that night or week as love gifts. We would wrap our baked goods up individually. We would take them with us when we would go out in the evenings to the bars. These small sweet treats would be given as a kind gesture to new bar owners. Many times it offered us an opportunity to come back. I got to know many new ladies and familiarize myself with so many bars and brothels through this simple act. It was amazing the magnitude that a small gesture, like a cookie, could make.

A new bar. A new girl. A first conversation. Soon, involvement in one of our programs. Next, possibly a job and a new life! It is simple acts of kindness that create open doors of opportunity. You never know who you will meet or where the path will lead you. Love's language is kindness. Kindness is a small, simple action.

We each have the power to choose.

chapter fifteen
THE SPIRIT WORLD

My experiences lead me to travel throughout Thailand. I found myself meeting others in the fight against sexual exploitation and trafficking. I have had the opportunity, not only to see different ways others are helping, but also to serve alongside them for days and weeks at a time. I am blown away by the creativity and uniqueness we all bring to the table. I am continually inspired by those that give their lives to fight for this cause. There are many commonalities I see in each establishment and every individual that chooses to walk this journey.

We share a common vocabulary. "Those ladies," or "those victims," or "that problem" is not part of our thoughts or speech. They are our "friends" and our "colleagues." We refer to them in these ways and terms. We love through the uncertainty, the mystery, the bleakness, the hopelessness, the unknown. It is a task we take on vigilantly. There can be no restoration if we are not willing to walk through the messiness and ugliness. We embrace the darkness and the brokenness. Our girls are not defined by what they do but by who they are.

We believe our girls are worth it and so much more! These were the small details I noticed. No one shared about it. I observed and found encouragement. I was being transformed. My thinking was shifting. It felt good to know there was a huge family of people operating the same way. I also observed some commonalities between methods, beliefs, and insights gained. I was encouraged that many of the things I had witnessed and many of my conclusions from those experiences were similar to theirs. Even though we had unique experiences and worked with different organizations we had so much in common.

These commonalities reinforced how much I had grown, gained, and learned over my years of experience. Coming from a small city in the heart of America, I had definitely crossed a vast ocean. The ocean held many, many struggles and dark times for me. Yet on the flip side, when the sun shone brightly and the sea was calm, I could see the light dancing on its glorious blue waves. I had crossed the ocean. Visiting these other organizations was like standing on the other side enjoying the view. I had been there and done that. I was not the same girl who had started.

I bounced along, uncomfortably hot. The windows were all down and the wind blew hot air on my face. It was too loud to talk. I was seated with my teammates on a bus. We were thirty minutes away from Bangkok. I found myself excited. I wondered what I might find. I remember holding my suitcase as I walked up a very narrow staircase. As we walked, our host was sharing. My ears perked up when she said they had a ninety-nine percent success rate. That was almost perfect! That meant that girls that came out of prostitution or had been rescued from sex trafficking did not find themselves back in its ugly grasp. In my experience, this high of a success rate was very rare.

What were they doing? What was different?

My curiosity was getting the best of me again.

I soon found myself in a big room. There were long tables lined in neat rows. The chairs were filled with Thai girls. There were at least thirty girls in the room. The room was quiet. Each girl was busily focused on the task in front of her. I circled the room slowly as I listened. Our host would stop and explain what different girls were doing. Each girl was putting together jewelry. There were wire and beads everywhere. She explained that this was a business.

The girls were employed by the business. We were shown the punch cards and lunch break room.

I was honored to meet the jewelry designer who happened to be visiting there that week. It was amazing learning about the inside of a business. She had actually helped market the jewelry to some big department stores in the U.S.A. She was back helping the staff gear up for the big rush of Christmas sales! It filled my heart with so much happiness to know that there would be legitimate sales.

We were led back into the jewelry making room and introduced to the manager. She was a girl who had been rescued and had worked her way up to the position. While in the room, there was a loud shriek and commotion. The girl making the noise was helped out of the room and we were also ushered out.

Soon we found ourselves in another room waiting to meet the founder. A foreign lady greeted us. I wondered about the commotion I had just witnessed. Pleasantly, I got an answer. I believe they didn't want us to worry. I was not prepared for her explanation.

The founder began sharing they were a faith-based organization with a legal and licensed business. They kept the lines separated, yet found and believed that both components created their high success rate. The girls that wanted a job with them also had other requirements to fulfill. She continued to explain how it was important to meet the needs of the whole person. They focused on the emotional, the physical, and the spiritual side of each individual.

Having actual jobs, for these women, is the first step in creating a new life. The girls were given a place to live. Most of them lived on-site. Their living was more like a "mentorship recovery facility." The girls stayed in this type of housing until they had enough money to live on their own. The girls were required to be part of certain activities that involved their growth emotionally and mentally.

They had curfews and wake up times. There were also accountability partners that they had to meet with. There were instances when an individual was not safe if left alone. Other stories were shared about girls sneaking out and going back into the scene. Our host even shared how they are extremely cautious about any of their girls seeing family members or friends. Many of these exchanges have ended or hampered the girls progress. I found this especially fascinating. Family members would convince or bring shame and fear on the girls for their choices. Sometimes it would be this contact that would have them sneak off! It made sense to me. I recounted all the girls I had met whose family members and friends were the very ones who recruited or sold them off.

Emotionally, many of the girls were codependent and had many unhealthy tendencies from trauma. Our host explained the programs they offered. It was mandatory for each of the girls to participate in these programs. The programs involved emotional help and healing from trauma. I was impressed with the enormity of their operation. I knew firsthand the complexity involved to tackle each of these areas. I also knew how courageous the girls in the program were.

What a huge undertaking they stepped into. I learned that they each worked eight-hour shifts, went to their counseling, and met with their accountability partners. All this while maintaining strict curfews and following precise rules. It was extremely controlled. However, the owners did not seem controlling. There was a feeling of love and compassion. Finally we got back to what the commotion was all about.

I stared back in disbelief. I myself had come to similar conclusions, but this was the first time I had heard anyone validate my own observations, let alone speak about it...publicly! Our host shared that the girl who left the room was demon possessed! *What?* It wasn't exactly what I imagined she would say, but I was curious. Coming from a religious background I was familiar with the term and many explanations behind it. I braced myself for the worst. Many times, faith-based organizations can be very judgmental in their spiritual interpretations toward mysterious encounters. It involves their way of interpreting faith. I found myself surprised, in a good way. Not only that, it connected some dots in my own experience.

Our host explained that many of the girls were dedicated to spirits and gods as babies and children. I knew this was true in my own personal experience and study of Thai culture and Buddhism. I listened on. Sometimes there were even ceremonies done over them when they were sold or given to pimps. I had never heard that before. My mind connected more dots. This could very well happen as many parents were the ones to sell their children into the industry knowingly and unknowingly. These gods or lords have control over the individual she continued to explain.

This may sound completely foreign to a westerner, but for a Thai this is a true fact and normal. What I found fascinating was how she began to connect this to being part of the reason why some of these girls continue back into the cycle and cannot stay away. My mind began going into overdrive! I started to connect things in my own experience. The devotion I saw in the girls I worked with. The extreme actions they would do to appease the spirits. The vigilance they had. If anyone would ever ask me, I would say they are some of the most spiritual people I have ever met.

She continued on, saying that many of these demons or lords had control over their minds and bodies. Until the curses spoken on or over them were broken, the girls would not find true or full restoration. I know there may be many who find it all "hokey pokey," the very idea, yet it resonated in my heart! It felt like the key to unlock something. I had never met anyone before who had talked about this topic. My husband and I would spend hours sorting through it. I, however, had never seen someone take the spiritual information of the people and use it for healing and restoration! My heart leaped. I felt this was a road that not many had walked. Maybe this was the true key in success?

In most of Asia, spirits, ghost, and the unseen world plays a huge part in the physical world. I have found that curses, poverty, evil spirits, and ghosts haunt, torment, and keep many of my friends bound in their grasp. Their own belief says that poverty, loss, death, and any other thing that are not good come from bad spirits. Good spirits bring success, happiness, and life. Whether one believes in the spirit world or not, to work with a population that does believe in it and never address it, leaves a huge vacant hole. I am inclined to believe that if a girl believes in these things, then it is very necessary to address them.

I found this organization did just that. They tackled the spiritual component head on. They did not push their religion onto the ladies. They simply learned what the ladies believed and found a solution! Many of my friends spent so much time praying and giving ohms to the spirits out of fear. Fear that they would make the spirit unhappy. Fear that anything good in their life would get ruined. I found it truly beautiful that this organization was addressing the girls' very real, felt fear.

I read once the opposite of fear is love. I truly believe love is a spirit. Love looks and feels a certain way. Love brings hope and healing. Love fights against fear and evil. Love always wins. I am inclined to believe if the actual girl believes in these things then it is very necessary to address them also. They simply learned what the ladies believed and used it as part of their healing process of transformation! I was so impacted by that conversation I immediately went up to speak to the lady when she finished her talk.

Boldly I asked her how she went about working through the Thai beliefs, curses and spirits. I wanted something practical. Something that I could actually do. She motioned me to follower her. As we walked through the hallways I began to share. My husband is a Christian. He is a missionary, pioneer and church planter. His methods are very unconventional. Seventeen years in Thailand has guided him on his unique path. The Thai he works with do not know he is a Christian. To them, he is a medium—a spiritual person of power. He has a spirit that lives inside of him. When he goes into villages and homes throughout Thailand, he is treated with honor and respect. He prays blessing over individuals and families, chanting in Buddhist rhythms. I shared some of the commonalities my husband had seen involving curses and blessings with what she was describing with me. We continued on in mutual understanding with story after story of the reality of the spirit world in Thailand. Once we arrived at an office, she pulled out a drawer and handed me a stack of papers.

The stack was large—at least two inches thick! She explained that in those papers were every spirit and demon they had come in contact with through the girls they worked with! Each account had the details recorded. Details included the type of curse that was given and the words that were spoken to break it. The type of ceremony that was performed and the name of the spirit involved was also written down! I cradled the stack of papers like it was money. Currency in this very specific journey. In that moment, I felt I had just won the lottery! I still have that stack of papers and refer to it often. That trip opened up a new world to me. It confirmed to me the important role that spirituality plays in humans. My time at this organization also convinced me that true success only happened when the entire person was attended to. The emotional, mental, physical, and spiritual needs were all equally important.

There are so many layers. Each layer must be valued and worked through to get to the heart of modern-day slavery. I felt like I was peeling layers. I felt my experiences had gently and gradually taken me on a spiral down to the heart. I believe peeling back each layer paved a way in understanding what complete restoration looked like and involved for the ladies that had become my friends. They were not just a number. They were valuable, beautiful. They were worth the intentional effort of adjusting my own beliefs. They were worth the effort of researching and understanding new religions. They were worth the effort of believing something I knew so little about. They were worth the effort of diving into the spirit world.

I went out to a brothel with this new organization. We left while it was still light outside. It was too dangerous to go very late. We pushed our way through crowded streets. The toxic heat seared my skin and as I breathed, the stringent smells burned my nose. My eyes watered from the smog. The smog lays so heavy, the sky is grey. I felt that way that night. I felt a gloomy feeling, an overwhelming feeling. Being in a huge city has a way of making me feel tiny. I felt our efforts were so small. How could I, how could we make a dent in this issue? I pondered what I had seen and all I had learned that day as I walked. I walked past drunk girls being guided away and wasted men yelling slurs and comments. I felt gut-wrenching sorrow. I felt despair. That all disappeared when I looked up and saw our guide. One girl, who had braved through her horrendous experience of sexual exploitation and had journeyed to the other side of restoration and healing. She represented the "other side."

In some weird way, it triggered all the stories of hope I had heard that day—the courageous journey of many other girls that had found restoration and healing after being rescued. I began to focus on my own journey, a journey that involved myself stepping out into the unknown. The things I had observed and learned through my own experiences. The way my mind had begun to shift. I smiled as I thought about all the ways I had grown as a person. Rubbing shoulders with individuals trapped in modern-day slavery changed me. I had set out to change the world but found I was the one impacted and changed the most. Maybe the first step to seeing any change involves awareness of our own limitations and the beginning steps of transforming those. I find as I change, I become a change agent. It is not something I have to work at. It is something I become.

The more I am exposed to, the more aware I am. No one has to tell me their story in detail. I know each of us has been through something. Our stories are different but they all share pain, disappointment, and hurt. I do know one thing—love has no borders. It is not for the rich or for those who have it all figured out or even for the hyper-spiritual. Love is for everyone and can be felt by everyone. We all are worthy of love. In my own life, I have found that the depth of pain, suffering, and despair I have felt is also the depth of love I have experienced. They are like yin and yang. We cannot have one without the other. They co-exist. I have found that in a place of darkness, it is hard to see the light and my eyes can only see my pain. The challenge I have each day is choosing to see the light, keeping my eyes glued on love.

Modern-day slavery is a global epidemic. I am so thankful that more light is being shed on the topic. It is not a centralized issue in the red light districts of the world, but reaches every country, every nationality, every age, gender, and you may be surprised that it even touches your own neighborhood. I have been face to face with the enormous, overwhelming, massive issue of exploitation in our world. Many times, it happens right in front of us without us ever having any idea about it. Women and children living in abusive, devaluing homes. Cultures that accept exploitation and abuse as normal. Societies that never address the inhumane and dehumanizing beliefs that have been carried on from generation to generation. The cycle is sickening. It has generations of momentum behind it. History speaks of its far-stretching arms. In every country, there are examples; from slavery to female mutilation to children brides. The list is long and the issues complex.

Until we are aware and accept it, in all its ugliness, for what it is, change will be slow. Until we embrace our own ugliness—the stereotypes, prejudices, and beliefs that keep us from embracing one another, we will not see change. Change occurs when we sit in our own mess, embrace our own ugliness and faults, and out of that, resolve to change. Out of the depth of that revelation, we can grow. I believe we must become the change that we want to see. Restored, whole, and alive. Embrace the darkness and soon a light will shine on a path out.

chapter sixteen

ARRANGED MARRIAGE

On one of my days off, I found myself sitting in a nail salon.

Usually, it's a silent retreat for me and I tend to close my eyes and enjoy the massage chair and the pampering. On this day, I could not take my eyes off the woman sitting in the chair next to me. She was beautiful. She looked to be around my same age. I noticed she had a henna tattoo covering her hands and climbing up her arms. She was dressed in the traditional Indian sari. I could tell this one was special. It was covered in gold. Her wrists were adorned in stacks of bangles. Her fingers showcased multiple gold rings. Around her neck she wore tons of gold necklaces, all layered, varying in size and length. She had bangles on her ankles that had little bells. The bells would ring any times she moved. She looked like a modern-day princess.

I had this huge urge inside of me to *know* her. I really wanted to talk to her. I felt deep down we could be good friends. I had never had an Indian friend before. As I sat getting my own nails done, I stole away glances in her direction trying not to look like I was eavesdropping! As I watched the most ornate decorated nails being done, I finally mustered my courage and asked if she spoke English. She did! We spent the next thirty minutes chatting away.

I learned that Kay was in her final preparation for her wedding. Her wedding was a week-long affair. I was super excited for her. I loved a good romance. I found myself assuming she had some amazing proposal as part of the story. I started putting questions in the safe box of my brain to ask later. All my questions suddenly seemed unimportant and obsolete when she told me that her marriage was arranged! I was more shocked when she said she had never met her husband before! Not only that, but she had just arrived in Thailand that week. The beautiful, romantic story I had envisioned in my head burst in an instant! I didn't have time to think of questions. Kay continued her story without missing a beat.

Her soon to be husband and his family had been

living in Thailand for generations. His parents' family, back in India, knew her parents' family. This was how the connection and arrangement started. I learned that there is a huge Indian population in Thailand, a small fact I had never known before. The Indians that live here never interracially marry. They would only marry other Indians.

These Indian families would also send their children away to boarding schools back in India. This way, the child would learn the language and customs of their people. Once the child finished school, it was expected of them to then move back to Thailand to take over their parents' business. This created strong cultural attachments. I was immersed in the details. This was so fascinating to me.

When I asked my new friend Kay how she felt about an arranged marriage, she had no qualms about it. She was more nervous about being in a new place alone, without her family and friends. I could tell this was an acceptable scenario. To my friend Kay, it was normal and nothing seemed out of place in her world. I listened on.

I have found, in my own experience of being married internationally, there were many relational things that I took for granted. I assumed some things were right and some things were wrong.

Yet, in many cultures, my husband's included, they are not a right or wrong issue, but merely a survival tactic or a matter of fact "this is the way we do it" scenario.

I remember arguing with my husband that it was not right for a spouse to live in another country. In my opinion, it could not be classified as a good, happy marriage. I truly believed that there must have been some sort of unhealthiness involved. I could not fathom a "good marriage" that involved a life of long distance. It seemed wrong to me. He shot back that families all over lived that way. It had nothing to do with health. Many times it has everything to do with wanting something better. He shared how many parents sacrifice spending time with their children for having a better paying job. This thought had never crossed my mind. I began to see how narrow my thinking was. I had never truly been immersed in a situation that would require that. What would I do if my children needed food on the table and the only job I could get was out of country? Many countries do not have job opportunities. Living in southeast Asia and marrying internationally has opened my eyes and my mind to these realities and choices parents have to face each day.

So many parents will travel overseas to find work. They even sacrifice seeing their children grow up by sending them away to boarding school. When I first became aware of this, it felt wrong to me. How could someone send their children away for their whole life. It seemed the opposite of love, from my view. The thought curled my stomach. I have since slowly learned to see, many do it out of love. They wanted the best opportunities and lives for their children.

We are all looking for something better. Our experiences are unique to each of us. We each take the opportunities presented in front of us. We hope they will bring us something better on this path of life.

My friend Kay shared how the marriage match was good for both families and how she was part of making that happen. I could see her unwavering spirit. She was a strong woman, with a strong moral compass and strong family ties. I am forever and always drawn to the strength of women. Sometimes it is the last thing they know about themselves. Every bone in my body see it and feels it. Kay was all things strong and beautiful.

She lit up every room she walked into. Her smile was electrifying and her heart made of gold. That day, sitting in the nail salon, we exchanged numbers. I could not wait to meet up again! I did not know when that would be. Kay said she did not have a car and would have to get permission to leave. She also shared that I was also not allowed to come over, because it was not her family. We would have to meet in a neutral spot.

Lastly, I was given strict orders not to call her–ever. She would call me.

The urgency in her voice as she relayed all of these requests raised some red flags in my mind. I did not know what to make of them. I could not have understood the fullness of her request at the time. I had just met her. I did not know the depths of her life. I had learned to not judge. I did not know what life was like in her culture. I had never walked in her shoes. At that moment, she seemed happy and that was all that mattered to me.

I thought about Kay often. Time ticked away. I thought we had hit it off. Maybe she didn't feel that way. I contemplated calling her. Her number glared back at me from my phone screen. I remembered her anxious request. *Don't call me, I will call you.* I felt responsible to honor her wishes. I waited and wondered. Time marched on.

Two months later, I got a phone call that was rushed and hushed. Whispering, Kay told me she would be at the grocery store in town at a certain time and asked for me to meet her. She immediately hung up. I felt panicked! What was going on? I had mixed emotions. I felt excitement that she called me and afraid at what it meant.

I wanted to know what was up. So, I did what she

asked and waited. She found me and together we walked through the shop. We found a small table and two chairs nestled in a corner and sat down together. In her cheerful demeanor and electrifying smile, she asked how I had been.

I didn't want small talk. I wanted to know how she was. Her first month with a husband she had never known before! She brushed it all off and said it was good. She emphasized how much she really missed her family. She was very lonely. Her in-laws would not let her leave the home. She was stuck inside with them day after long day. She described her living quarters to me. It seemed uncomfortable. They all lived together. Her and her new husband had a bedroom in the same house.

It seemed that just as quickly as we sat down, Kay was checking her watch and standing up, mumbling something about how she had to go now, but she would call and for me not to call. I kind of just sat there, watching. I didn't quite know what to do with it all. I felt in my spirit something wasn't right. She never let on about anything, though, so I had nothing to go with. I would just have to wait.

Another two months later, I got a phone call from Kay. I still didn't understand our dynamic. I felt like we hit it off really well. Why would she take so long to call?

Did she not like me? These insecure thoughts would circle my mind often. I had this thought that maybe we just didn't connect. She had probably found other friends.

When I got this phone call, she apologized for the distance. She had been really busy. Now she was free and she wanted to see me and meet up, this time for lunch. I remember eating curry with noodles. The dish is one of my favorites. I only took one bite, because I was so preoccupied with our conversation that my food went virtually untouched.

When we met for lunch, we had a great time catching up. With excitement, she shared that she was pregnant! This was a great thing! In her culture, this was the next thing that needed to happen after marriage. It was really good for my friend as it didn't take too long! She had only been married for a couple of months. It was a win for her and her new family.

She described to me how the families would make them go to their room so many times throughout the day. The weeks would go by with this treatment. I could see how humiliated and embarrassed she felt by this as she shared. Why she told me, I will never know. Her strength and courage was inspiring to me. She found great satisfaction and relief with the news of her pregnancy. I rejoiced with her. Her life could now be out of the spotlight in that way.

Indian culture is much like many other cultures I am intimately aware of. When a woman marries into another family, that family becomes her family and responsibility. It is her new role to take care of them, perform most of the housekeeping duties, and provide offspring. I have even heard it stated in extremely blunt terms that the wives of husbands become the slaves of their in-laws. That is the feeling I got when I was listening to my friend Kay. She never complained or even mentioned hardship. Her only issue involved the family never letting her out of their sight. She was not allowed to leave the house or go anywhere unchaperoned. Her family was usually shopping at the location we were meeting and she would steal away for a few minutes to be with me.

As we parted, I hugged and congratulated her. I will never forget the words she spoke as we parted.

With depth and calm, she looked me in the eyes and said, "You are the only friend I have and the only person I knew to share my happy news with." After that, she was gone again.

I wanted more from the relationship. I felt a deep sense of loyalty that involved not overstepping my boundaries. I waited and hoped for another phone call. The next one came five months later.

She was crying when I answered. She tried to talk but was overcome with sobs and then she hung up. My stomach dropped. My mind bolted! What was going on? A day later, another phone call. This time she sounded happy and in a good mood. She asked to meet at our spot in the grocery store later that week. Before she could hang up, I quickly asked if everything was okay. She convinced me that it was and said we would talk when we met up.

I waited at our table, my thoughts wandering, and I found myself making my own hypotheses. It's funny how we do that, creating some sort of scenario before we know the facts. Soon, I was interrupted by a gentle hand brushing my shoulder. Excitement rose up inside of me as I turned and saw my friend. Those feelings vanished just as fast, as I noticed my friend nervously looking from side to side and behind her.

Once she sat down, I noticed a bruise on her cheek. Before I could even ask, she fearfully shared she couldn't stay long. She was here with family and couldn't get away for more than a few minutes without raising suspicion. Then, as a volcano sitting dormant, she erupted with such force, it sucked my breath right out of me. Tears streamed down her face just as fast as her words rushed out. Her husband was beating her. I didn't know what to say. I didn't know what to do. I had never been faced with such a complex issue. One that involved culture, respect, and other layers I didn't know the first thing about. I was in a foreign land. I felt helpless. How could I help? What was the best approach? My thoughts raced.

I desperately wanted to help. My heart yearned to make her world a better place. The saddest part in the whole story was somehow he, her husband, had the right to do what he did. It crippled me as I heard her share from this point of view. She was worth so much more! Everything in my being wanted to protect her. I wanted to physically shelter her from the blows.

Her in-laws did nothing to protect her. The beatings had started at the five-month mark of her pregnancy. This was the exact time they found out the gender of the baby–a girl. I had no idea Indian culture was so partial to genders. I learned from my friend that it is a sign of good luck and great fortune to have a son first. This ensures the family name will be carried on to the next generation.

My friend continued in detail how the beatings would happen every night after her husband would come home. She would be pinned in her room, helpless, trapped, and pregnant. If she tried to escape her bedroom, her in-laws would be standing outside ready to forcefully stop her escape.

She sobbed as she shared her escape attempts. My heart ached. It felt so heavy. My own tears were running free. She tried to escape out of her bedroom window, only to have a family member waiting on the other side to usher her back inside. They were always watching. They never let her out of their sight.

She apologized for not calling. They took her phone from her. She had secretly stolen her husband's phone while he was asleep to call me the last time. I was not only devastated, I was angry! The injustice. The entrapment. The devaluing. I hated it! I hated the idea that a pregnancy gave this evil power leverage in her culture and family. A beautiful baby girl could, in fact, change that fortune. To me it was ridiculous. I couldn't understand it. How could a whole family participate in such assault?

She even shared that she knew her husband loved another girl—a Thai girl. He would leave a lot to spend time with her. She shared how she was so lonely, pregnant with her first child, far from home, and without a way to contact her family or friends. Her husband did not love her. It was his duty, culturally, as the oldest son, to marry an Indian girl and produce offspring. Preferably a boy. The baby was due in a couple weeks. She attempted to convince herself she was okay by telling me that after the baby was born, surely things would go back to normal. I was not so sure.

Our meeting was short. It lasted ten minutes. Yet those ten minutes felt like hours of information and insight. The fullness of the picture she painted has stuck with me for over a decade. She left distraught and afraid. The fear was so evident. She was going back into a very dangerous situation. As she rushed out, she whispered that she would call me when she could.

Sitting there, I had nowhere to turn. No police to call. No hotline to help. No organization that I knew of. The devaluing and dehumanizing of women curls my insides. It burns so deep inside of me. It is an injustice that I feel firsthand, as a woman, as a minority, and as an expat. It keeps me up at night. It torments my very being.

All I could imagine was the countless number of girls in these situations. Their fear. The loneliness they feel. The entrapment. Victims.

There were so many parallels between my friend Kay's life and experience and the girls I worked with in the red light districts. One thing that was different hit me really hard. Kay, and others like her, lived under nightmarish conditions that their entire society accepted as okay! An action based on cultural beliefs and a normal way of life.

How does one rescue, defend, and help someone in this situation? Especially if they themselves believe it is acceptable! I sat there contemplating it all over and over in my head. Did I do the right thing? Was it good to let her go? My decisions—and regrets—were on replay in my head. It took a long time for me to accept that I had done everything I could. I felt peace with that decision, but I walked away from that meeting devastated.

One never really knows what is going on behind closed doors. We all have a story. We all have gone, or will go, through something that will shake the very foundations we have always stood on. I know, in those times, all you do is try to keep your head above the water. Survive. However, you can, by whatever means you can. I have been there. Most days, breathing is a win...*check.*

Most of us will walk through life with a smile plastered on our face. We will engage in small talk with strangers and family, a survival method that fools everyone around us into thinking our life is good. Behind closed doors life can be bleak, murky, and dark.

Parts of our world are twisted. We say we want to help. We are infuriated. We want to fight injustice. We want racism and discrimination to stop. We say we believe women and children should have equal rights. We hit the "like" button for anything that pertains to this. Yet, our talk and our actions are separate. They are two different things.

We don't have time for people's problems. Their struggles are complicated and complex. The wounds are ugly. Hurting people hurt people. There is a stench of negativity, bitterness, blame. Each of these common denominators that are pieces of deep brokenness. On the outside, everything looks fine enough.

Looks are deceiving.

What is brought to the forefront is our own inability to empathize. We don't know how to be vulnerable. Let alone sit with and truly emphasize with someone who is vulnerable. Sharing violence and brokenness is a dark negative experience many of us find ways to dodge. We don't know how to ask for help. More importantly when someone screams "help" by sharing their stories of pain...we convince ourselves someone else is better equipped to help them. I have found in my own life as my awareness grew, my impact grew. I can only give what I have on the inside. What I have learned is that I can give time. I can empathize. I can embrace the ugly violent mess in those vulnerable enough to share their deepest darkest pain. I have learned to not give advice or answers. The simple act of presence is enough.

Love stops in the business and hurriedness of life. Love waits patiently, quietly listening. Its senses are heightened and love is ready to battle. Love stands up and defends. Love engulfs with a hug. Love drops everything, because nothing is more important than you. People matter. They are of the highest value. Inside of us there is unending potential. Unleashed, we are a force of beautiful change. Love does not prefer a gender, race, or religion. We are humanity. We are limitless. We are valuable.

My friend Kay had her baby; a beautiful, sweet little girl with rosy cheeks and curly brown hair. She was precious. My friend fell in love the moment she laid eyes on her. Over the next eight months, I saw my friend two times. She never let on about anything bad. We spent most of the time talking about her daughter. She was still watched. She still did not have freedom. The family-in-law seemed to appreciate her more because she brought new life to the home. This created excitement and happiness for the older generation. Her husband was still cheating on her. She assured me it did not bother her anymore. She had her daughter to focus on now.

I traveled stateside for the summer. My first day home, back in Thailand, I got an unexpected phone call. It was Kay! She wanted to meet! What perfect timing–I could not have planned it better myself. She seemed happy. I did not sense any fear. Convinced by her tone of voice, I began to get excited.

Once we met up, though, I was surprised that her daughter was not with her and asked about her. Immediately, her countenance changed–her shoulders slumped, her eyes looked away and down. I braced myself. *No! Not again!* My mind screamed. I clenched my chair with my fist.

My friend had been able to contact her parents in India, six months ago. They had wired her money to get out and fly back home. The abuse had started back up. It was happening daily. She shared how it was getting worse because her husband wanted another child. A boy this time. With money and the blessing of her family in India, she made a plan of escape. She tried multiple times and multiple ways. Each time was unsuccessful. Each time ended in a brutal beating. I could barely continue listening. Tears streamed down my face. How strong she was. How brave she was.

One day, while out with her family at the grocery store, she got away for a few minutes using the same tactics she would use to meet with me. During this brief time, she met an older Australian couple. She confided in them a bit and they gave her their phone number. If she needed anything, they said to call.

After countless failed attempts, my friend mustered enough strength to try again. This time, as she grabbed her daughter to make an exit, her mother-in-law yanked the baby from her arms. My friend paused as she described the two of them facing each other...eyes locked. I could only imagine the intense situation. What was my friend thinking? What would she do? As Kay stood paralyzed watching her daughter cry, her mother-in-law gave her a choice: stay here with your daughter or leave without her. My heart sank. I didn't want to think. It was so devastating. My friend couldn't live with that choice! We were both crying now. Between sobs, my friend shared about the yelling, the begging, the sobbing, how she got down on her knees and pleaded with her mother-in-law. It was all to no avail. Then, in a final act of desperation, my friend lunged at her daughter and a literal tug of war ensued! My friend looked at me with such defeat. Her eyes answered my questions. She couldn't get her free. The pain in her voice, the shame she carried—I wanted it to go away. I could see she felt like she had failed her daughter. My insides ached. In a split second, my friend had left the only thing that mattered to her. Her wounds were raw. It was painful to talk about. It was ugly.

Once she left, she had nowhere to go. She did not know anyone. She had no place to stay. She borrowed a phone and called the Australian couple. That was where she was staying now. She had been staying with them for three weeks. During those past three weeks, she had been trying to figure out a way to get her daughter so she could catch a plane and fly back to India, but nothing had worked. Her plane was leaving in a couple hours. I could tell my friend could not talk about the finality of that choice. It was too painful in that moment. She was trying to survive. Trying to hope. We embraced for a long time. I knew I might never see her again.

I do not even remember anything I said during that time. I was relieved and heartbroken. My friend boarded that plane with so much bravery. Her will, fight and determination was so admirable, so challenging, so beautiful. In the depths of despair and pain, I saw beauty. Her fight mirrored to me that of a caterpillar in a cocoon fighting and wrestling to see a brighter day. I wanted so badly for her to have happiness instead of mourning. I hoped she would find strength and restoration. I prayed she would somehow be reunited with her daughter and that the black ash of her life would one day birth something beautiful.

I usually get a phone call twice a year from my friend Kay in India. We are friends on social media and continue to stay in touch. My friend and her parents went to court in India and prosecuted her husband. They won! He is "red flagged" and would be arrested and thrown into jail if he ever tried to step foot back in India. My friend was never able to get her daughter back. She loves her fiercely and has tried countless ways to get her back, a fight I am sure she will continue until she dies.

It has been eight years since that fateful day she left on a plane, leaving her daughter behind. I have seen from afar her ex-husband and daughter walking through the mall a few times over the years. Her daughter grows more and more beautiful each passing year. Every time I see her, my heart is so heavy and my mothering side comes out with a vengeance. My oldest son is one year younger than her daughter. I could never imagine what my friend Kay has been through.

When I get a glimpse of her daughter around town, I am always so excited to relay what I saw to Kay when I get that random phone call. It took my friend a long time to recover. It took her some time to assimilate back to normal life in India.

I learned that she moved to another city on her own, four months after arriving. The shame she brought to her family, divorcing and leaving her husband, was too much. Even though her parents were supportive of her, the backlash they received from their family and community was too overwhelming. My friend found a job and started a new life. She got married a couple years ago and has a sweet little baby. There is always a new day. A new chance. A new life that can be had.

May every girl that is exploited have the opportunity to be *not just a number*. I hope they each find someone to invest in them. Someone to believe in them. Someone who will walk with them and carry their pain. May they have a second chance in life. May they experience restoration and healing. May their name forever be imprinted on someone's heart, like Kay's is on mine. They are valuable. They matter. May all of us let love guide.

If we do this, I believe we will see how it demolishes stereotypes. We will see how love triumphs over evil. We will experience how hope will champion the weak. When all things fail, love will shelter and protect those who are suffering. Love is loyal, victorious, healing, and kind, gentle in its ways and bold in its moves. Love never backs down in messy situations, but defends the vulnerable. It is the beauty in the darkness, the wind in our sails. It is the hope in hopelessness and the light in darkness. Love wins. Love heals. Love restores.

Love says they are not just a number. You are not just a number. I am not just a number.

DEAR READER

It is with great humility and honor that I thank you for being *Not Just a Number*.

All proceeds from this book will go toward the fight against slavery.

Your contribution will make a difference as together we shine a light on human exploitation and sex trafficking.

Modern-Day Slavery
Global Statistics

After reading, you may have found yourself wanting more information concerning sexual exploitation and human trafficking in today's world. Sex trafficking is defined as the illegal business of recruiting, harboring, transporting, obtaining, or providing a person and especially a minor for the purpose of sex.[1]

You may be asking yourself, "What can I do? What is next?"

Maybe you just want some more information.

Here, I have outlined statistics for human trafficking and exploitation from 2014 to 2017.

1. *"Sex Trafficking." Merriam-Webster's Collegiate Dictionary.* 11th ed. Springfield, MA: Merriam-Webster, 2003. Also available at http://www.merriam-webster.com/.

Look at the trends, see the numbers—numbers that should not exist. Take action and be the change you wish to see. In 2014, 21 million people globally were estimated to be trapped in modern-day slavery. The image below depicts how modern-day slavery has become a global epidemic.[2]

21 million people victims of forced labour

Based on research in 2014, Southeast Asia and the Pacific vastly outnumber the other regions by holding the majority of victims.

2. "Statistics on Forced Labour, Modern Slavery and Human Trafficking." International Labour Organization. Accessed November 08, 2017. http://www.ilo.org/.

Southeast Asia and the Pacific are where all of my experiences come from. The most common form of human trafficking is sexual exploitation (79%).

The victims of sexual exploitation are predominantly women and girls.

In my own experience—and this is concurrent with modern research—many will find it surprising that women trafficking women is often times the norm!

Sexual exploitation, sometimes known as "sex tourism," is a 150 billion dollar industry.

The second most common form of human trafficking is forced labor (18%). Although, this may be a misrepresentation because forced labor is less frequently detected and reported than trafficking for sexual exploitation.

Nearly 20% of all trafficking victims are children.[3] That is around 5.5 million children worldwide.[4]

3. "United Nations Office on Drugs and Crime." Global Report on Trafficking in Persons. Accessed November 9, 2017. http://www.unodc.org/unodc/en/human-trafficking/global-report-on-trafficking-in-persons.html

4. "Humanitarian Aid for Children in Crisis." UNICEF USA. Accessed November 9, 2017. https://www.unicefusa.org/.

In November 2017 during the UN General Assembly, the International Labour Organization and Walk Free Foundation announced the largest ever assembly of statistical data and current estimates on human trafficking.

Below is data from The Global Slavery Index in 2016.[5]

The magnitude of victims suffering from modern-day slavery increases every year!

5. Global Slavery Index. Accessed December 02, 2017.

https://www.globalslaveryindex.org/country/united-states/.

As of November 2017, human trafficking is still the largest form of sexual exploitation at 99%.[6] Compared to data from 2014, that is a 20% increase! Southeast Asia may be the most well-known locale for human trafficking, but data shows that our world is digressing.

Per UNICEF, Trafficking involves:

pornography
sex tourism
forced marriage
prostitution
sweatshop work
forced armed services
migrant farming
and begging

Dare to dream and know that you *can* do something.

6. 2017 Global Estimates of Modern Slavery and Child Labour. Accessed December 03, 2017. http://www.alliance87.org/2017ge/.

I hope this book filled you with every emotion possible. I hope you feel that I did my friends justice in portraying their insurmountable courage that continues to inspire me. I hope that as you finished the last page, you yearned for more.

Friends, there is so much more.

Though you may feel ordinary and you lack knowledge or skills, I hope that my journey inspires and ignites you to take action! You can make a difference in someone's life—that someone may be trapped in one of the biggest global epidemics in our world today.

So what can you do?

Sign up for my FREE end it movement action plan.

www.nekieshalynn.com

This book is dedicated to the "End It Movement," a coalition of leading organizations in the fight for freedom.

This book is my contribution to shine a light on slavery.

1. "Sex Trafficking." Merriam-Webster's Collegiate Dictionary. 11th ed. Springfield, MA: Merriam-Webster, 2003. Also available at http://www.merriam-webster.com/.

2. "Statistics on Forced Labour, Modern Slavery and Human Trafficking." International Labour Organization. Accessed November 08, 2017. http://www.ilo.org/.

3. "United Nations Office on Drugs and Crime." Global Report on Trafficking in Persons. Accessed November 9, 2017.
http://www.unodc.org/unodc/en/human-trafficking/gloal-report-on-trafficking-in-persons.html

4. "Humanitarian Aid for Children in Crisis." UNICEF USA. Accessed November 9, 2017. https://www.unicefusa.org/.

5. Global Slavery Index. Accessed December 02, 2017.
https://www.globalslaveryindex.org/country/united-states/.

6. 2017 Global Estimates of Modern Slavery and Child Labour. Accessed December 03, 2017. http://www.alliance87.org/2017ge/.

ACKNOWLEDGMENTS

I want to thank my husband and two sons, Tele and Losi, for loving me unconditionally and walking hand in hand with me through this journey.

I want to thank the "End It" movement coalition and the work they have done in the fight for freedom.

I want to thank Lifegate Church Omaha Nebraska for ten years of deep, loving and meaningful relationship—financially, emotionally and spiritually. In a place surrounded by differences and unfamiliarity, I found home and belonging with you.

I want to thank Mark and Christa Crawford for giving me a chance that paved a way for my own personal transformation on this journey.

ABOUT THE AUTHOR

Nekiesha Lynn is a humanitarian, a public speaker, a woman, a wife, a mother, and a champion for those most vulnerable amongst us. For the past decade Nekiesha Lynn has helped and advocated for her amazing friends trapped in and coming out of modern-day slavery in South East Asia.

She has a BA degree in Communications and minor in Buddhism. She currently lives and works between Thailand and the United States with her husband and her two sons.

Nekiesha Lynn is an anti-trafficking activist and a passionate "End It" advocate. With *Not Just a Number*, Nekiesha Lynn hopes to shine a light on slavery.

Sign up for my FREE end it movement action plan.

www.nekieshalynn.com